Marriage Maintenance

Better to Repair Than to Replace

TYRONE HOLCOMB

CREATION
HOUSE

MARRIAGE MAINTENANCE by Tyrone Holcomb
Published by Creation House
A Charisma Media Company
600 Rinehart Road
Lake Mary, Florida 32746
www.charismamedia.com

Unless otherwise noted, all Scripture quotations are from the King James Version of the Bible.

Scripture quotations marked THE MESSAGE are from *The Message: The Bible in Contemporary English*, copyright © 1993, 1994, 1995, 1996, 2000, 2001, 2002. Used by permission of NavPress Publishing Group.

Scripture quotations marked NCV are from The Holy Bible, New Century Version. Copyright © 1987, 1988, 1991 by Word Publishing, Dallas, Texas 75039. Used by permission.

Scripture quotations marked NLT are from the Holy Bible, New Living Translation, copyright © 2007. Used by permission of Tyndale House Publishers, Inc., Wheaton, IL 60189. All rights reserved.

Scripture quotations marked TLB are from The Living Bible. Copyright © 1971. Used by permission of Tyndale House Publishers, Inc., Wheaton, IL 60189. All rights reserved.

Scripture quotations marked NIV are from the Holy Bible, New International Version of the Bible. Copyright © 1973, 1978, 1984, 2011 by Biblica, Inc. Used by permission.

Unless otherwise noted, all chapter-opening quotes have been taken from *BrainyQuote* at BrainyQuote.com.

The author and publisher have attempted to find every source quoted in this book. Any information found after this printing will be included during the first reprint.

Design Director: Justin Evans
Cover design by Terry Clifton

Visit the author's website: tyroneholcomb.com.

Library of Congress Cataloging-in-Publication Data:
2014948482
International Standard Book Number: 978-1-62136-806-9
E-book International Standard Book Number:
978-1-62136-807-6

While the author has made every effort to provide accurate telephone numbers and Internet addresses at the time of publication, neither the publisher nor the author assumes any responsibility for errors or for changes that occur after publication.

First edition

15 16 17 18 19 — 9 8 7 6 5 4 3 2 1
Printed in Canada

Contents

Foreword

IT SEEMS THAT each day of our lives we are inundated with new products we're told to buy, new music we should hear, or new books we should read. The sheer volume of these appeals makes it easy for us to dismiss most if not all of them in an effort to free up the mental shelf space we know we're going to need right around the corner.

But every now and then God allows for the release of an uncommon and extraordinary rendering of wisdom and insight that comes from being close to His heart. This book, *Marriage Maintenance*, is all of that and more.

While we all know marriage is honorable, many don't know that marriage can be wonderful. This leads some to conclude that marriage is disposable when instead marriage is repairable. Elder Tyrone Holcomb uses his unique and powerful anointing to reduce to simplicity the complexity of marriage into practical parts and workable solutions to make marriage manageable, not miserable.

I personally believe that for many, this book is a literal answer to prayer. As you journey through the pages of this book of wisdom regarding the mechanics of marriage maintenance, do so with an open heart and mind. You will laugh; you will cry—and everything in between.

Most of all you'll be given God's insight for your oversight of a marriage made in heaven—yours.

Forever leaning on Jesus,

—PASTOR ANTHONY WALLACE
CROSSROAD CHRISTIAN CHURCH

Acknowledgments

EVERYONE WHO PLAYED a part in this book's completion, thank you!

The reader, I pray this book takes you beyond deliverance to development.

Christian House of Prayer, I'm thankful and grateful to be numbered with you.

Olga Wise, my words aren't adequate enough to express my sincere appreciation for your gift of writing and passion toward this project.

Ramona Johnson, I admire your editorial prowess. I have learned much as we partner together on every book, and this one has been no exception.

My parents, you have been instruments in the Father's hand for my continual growth.

My children, I love each of you. Remember, progress is not an option; it's an obligation. The seeds I plant today will be the fruit for you tomorrow.

Andrea, my wife and friend, we are inextricably linked, and I will have it no other way. *I love you* because you give me every reason to.

My Lord, my greatest discovery is Your reality. You promised me Your presence, and where would I be without it?

Introduction

GREAT WORKS OF art are timeless, spanning the ages with their ability to capture the essence of a moment in time. Consider Michelangelo. With chisel in hand he captured the emotion and weight of Mary's sorrow at the death of her son, Jesus. He named his masterpiece the *Pietà*. Or, Henry Ossawa Tanner's *Banjo Lesson* uses the medium of a brush and paint to convey a grandfather's tender instruction, instilling the beauty of music into his grandson. We feel the strokes of a painter and the blows of a sculptor just by observing their works.

When acknowledging great works of art we must never forget that God Himself is *the* Virtuoso. Anyone who doubts that need only look at His many creations: the universe and its vast constellations and the Earth's various spheres, oceans, and landscapes. Last, humanity, with all its complexities and mystery, possesses God's greatest masterpiece, life itself.

The Maker took a blank canvas and with a stroke of genius created man and woman whose union would, by design, contain and convey God's very essence, love. Marriage, derived from the Holy and delivered to the human, is the dwelling He chose to house His love. *Therefore, marriage is a house of God's love.*

God, the master Architect of this house, designed it structurally sound and aesthetically beautiful. He thought so much about marriage He decided to have one Himself. On Mt. Sinai He married His chosen people with a band of unchanging moral principles called His covenant (Exod. 24:1–8).

Eventually the people of God defaced His land, disobeyed His laws, and doubted His love. Alas! The magnum opus of the marriage house was now marred. Nevertheless, God's greatest ability is His dependability. Even when we're faithless He's faithful. He didn't choose to replace His blemished bride but to repair her. God's marriage was not exempt from tests or trials, and neither is ours.

Many marriages are rendered condemned or, worse, facing demolition. However, the order to demolish has been changed to "polish." Before you knock down your marriage look up to the master Architect. God has the master plan for stunning success to help you and your spouse create a masterpiece of your own.

The goal of this book is to encourage you to remodel your marriage. A renewed marriage can experience excitement, enjoyment, and fulfillment. If your marriage foundation has shifted, that doesn't necessarily mean it's sinking; it could mean it's settling.

Therefore, I urge you: before you look to replace, learn how to repair and discover the power of marriage maintenance.

> Except the Lord build the house, they labour in vain that build it.
>
> —PSALM 127:1

THE FOUNDATION

The best way to find out if you can trust somebody is to
trust them.

—ERNEST HEMINGWAY

Chapter One

No Matter What

A MAN AND HIS daughter were crossing an old bridge on a cold, windy day. The little girl was apprehensive and unsure of their ability to cross safely, so she said to her father, "Daddy, please let me hold your hand; I'll feel safe and won't be afraid of falling." The father responded in a reassuring tone, "No, precious, let me hold your hand."

Baffled, the daughter inquired, "What difference does it make?" "The difference is significant," the caring father responded. He went on to say, "If you hold my hand and become frightened, you might release your grip. However, if I hold your hand, my grasp is firm and secure no matter what."

The foundation of any relationship is trust. The substance of trust is not found in having an arrangement, but in honoring the agreement. When we hold the hand of our loved ones we give that blessed assurance, "I'll hold you up; I won't hold back; and you can hold me to it."

SUPPORT: I'LL HOLD YOU UP

> For if they fall, the one will lift up his fellow: but woe to him that is alone when he falleth; for he hath not another to help him up.
> —ECCLESIASTES 4:10

Again, trust is the foundation in every relationship. If the foundation is suspect, nothing will remain on it for long. On the other hand, when the foundation is strong it will hold up or support anything. Couples need a firm foundation to establish a good relationship. If their trust for one another is strong, their bond will reflect it. However, the contrary is true also. Weak or little trust stifles and neuters the union.

Upon having our house built, Andrea and I were extremely

excited. Many days were consumed with planning. We spent countless hours exploring the house's amenities. We discussed the features, colors, and of course, the cost.

Once the construction of the house began we would visit the site every day. The first week we saw nothing but a lot of dirt. The second week, we spotted a dirt mound. The third and fourth week, to our discouragement, the mound became a mountain. I begin to think, "Maybe our dream house will be an outhouse."

As we visited the site in the second month of construction we discovered our dirt was now a ditch. We had never been so excited about seeing dirt moved around in our lives. We celebrated progress taking place. Within the next several weeks it appeared nothing was happening.

Finally, I inquired about the delay. The project manager informed me there was no delay, and in fact, they were right on schedule. Totally surprised, I asked him to explain. At that point I received a thorough class on laying a foundation.

Like my house, marriages need a firm foundation. This is established through expressing and receiving trust. Interestingly, when the house is complete, the foundation is no longer seen; but make no mistake, it's there. So it is with trust. Trust is the invisible force that holds the union up as well as together.

Speaking of being held up, I painfully recall my wife Andrea getting rid of my favorite La-Z-Boy recliner. Her reasoning was rational but not welcomed. She argued that the color of my chair did not complement the decor in our den. She wanted coordination; I was seeking comfort. She desired fashion; I just wanted to flop.

Eventually I capitulated. It didn't take long to discover that although the new chair had the looks, it didn't invite the lazy. This new chair was too pretty, too prissy, and well, too Andrea. My old chair was huge, contoured for my body, and above all, it was able to support my weight.

The way I felt about my chair, spouses should feel concerning one another. I loved my chair because I could trust my chair. Trust conveys, "I'll hold you up." When we can hold the weight of our spouse without making them feel guilty for it, trust is fortified and our marriage solidified.

One of the messages I wish to express to Andrea is my support. You should desire to support your spouse as well. Did you know one of our greatest abilities is our dependability? It's uplifting to know you can depend on someone, especially when that someone is your spouse.

God gave a commandment to the high priest of old how he was to wear his holy garment (Exod. 39). First of all, he bore onyx stones on his shoulders with the names of the children of Israel engraved in them (Exod. 39:6–7). Second, he wore a breastplate that vaunted various stones across it. Also, each stone had the names of the tribes of Israel on them (Exod. 39:8–14).

The holy garment was to be a symbol of the high priest's duties. The names on the shoulders represented carrying the people. The names across the heart revealed a caring for the people. God wants us to hold one another up by carrying and caring. When this is accomplished trust is soon established, and the foundation of your relationship is being laid.

SERVE: I WON'T HOLD BACK

> Those of us who are strong and able in the faith need to step in and lend a hand to those who falter, and not just do what is most convenient for us. Strength is for service, not status. Each one of us needs to look after the good of the people around us, asking ourselves, "How can I help?"
>
> —ROMANS 15:1–2, THE MESSAGE

One of the most endearing love stories in the Bible is that of Boaz and Ruth. Theirs is a tale of romance and respect. To read how these two responded to one another's love is truly remarkable and admiring.

To admire their love is easy, and I find it remarkable because of their various differences. He was an aged man, while she was rather young. She grew up on the wrong side of the tracks, while he was wealthy enough to own the railroad. He ran an institute, and she ran destitute. The two were on opposite ends of society's pole in every respect.

Boaz was an upright, well-respected man who could have had just about any woman he desired. At that time, the town of Bethlehem was just recovering from a ten-year famine. Marrying Boaz would have been equivalent to hitting the lottery.

Of all the women Boaz could have chosen, what made him choose Ruth? Was it physical beauty? Physical attraction is certainly nice to have in a marriage. But, no. Could it have been her social status in the community? We already established she was not of aristocratic descent. I submit unto you that Boaz chose Ruth because she respected him. And out of her respect, she rendered her service.

Ruth's crowning characteristic was her ability and willingness to serve. After losing her first husband to death she was given the opportunity by her mother-in-law, Naomi, to return to her own family and begin a new life. Rather than opting to take the pathway of ease, Ruth took the straightway to servitude. She knew it would be difficult for a much older Naomi to survive on her own. Therefore, she decided to work in order to provide for their means.

Ruth offers one of the most compelling and compassionate vows of commitment recorded in the Bible. She gives this proclamation to her mother-in-law: "Where you go, I go; and where you live, I'll live. Your people are my people, your God is my god; where you die, I'll die" (Ruth 1:16–17, THE MESSAGE). In essence, Ruth expressed, "I won't hold back!" She made a commitment to serve the person she loved.

This gives us a wonderful example for married couples. Our hearts should truly desire to serve our marital companions every day. It's a shame, but some only serve their spouse on certain occasions, such as birthdays, Father's Day, Mother's Day, etc.

This brings to mind a particular story. One morning on old McDonald's farm a cow, chicken, and pig decided to have a meeting. They discussed how old McDonald had taken very good care of all the animals.

So, the three decided it would be great to make breakfast for the old farmer. The cow exclaimed, "I'll provide the milk!" The chicken shouted, "I'll give up the eggs!" At this point the pig yelled, "Wait a minute! To participate I'll have to give my life." This story helps us to see an equal commitment doesn't always equate to an equal sacrifice.

Our service should never be measured by what the other does but rather by the value we have for each other. We're not married to compete with one another but to complement each other.

I, for one, discovered the pleasure in service. Now, I'm not purporting that I spend my every moment thinking how I can serve my wife. (I'm not perfect.) Nevertheless, I do find doing things for Andrea brings out the best in her, and it strengthens the foundation of our marriage.

Serving your spouse can establish trust. Through providing assistance to them, they'll be able to see your care and concern. Resist the temptation to be self-absorbed and self-serving. When you serve, don't let it be perfunctory; serve with passion. You can disarm your spouse by serving them. This also shows you love and respect them.

Let's return to Ruth. Her commitment to serving Naomi brought her face-to-face with her future husband, Boaz. When we don't hold back and we serve with liberality, God gets involved. What can appear to be mere coincidence all the while could be God's divine providence.

The Bible conveys that Ruth just happened to come to the piece of land that her future husband owned (Ruth 2:3). Just as Ruth served Naomi, she now served Boaz. In fact, Naomi wisely advised Ruth how to approach Boaz in order to win his affection. She instructed Ruth to wait until Boaz was asleep and to go and lay at his feet. In their custom, laying at his feet indicated she was presenting herself as his servant (Ruth 3:3–4).

Ruth's actions touched the heart of Boaz. Thus, he was moved and motivated to marry her. At that moment the walls of differences that separated them came crumbling down. Boaz committed himself to serve Ruth just as she had done for him and others. His trust in Ruth sky-rocketed because he knew she had his best interest at heart.

Trust warms the cockles of the heart, and serving our spouse presents the opportunity for trust to develop. For many, serving others does not come naturally, and like many it took me some time to warm up to the idea.

As a youth I was taught my vowels, and when reciting them the *I* always came before the *U*. Well, it didn't take me long to adopt that order into my philosophy. It became custom to place the *I* before *you* in all my relationships. However, once I made a vow to my wife, the *you* needed to take precedence over the *I*. I had to learn not to hold back my service to my wife.

Doing this made it possible for her to trust me and reciprocate the favor. Our service must not come with ulterior motives. It must come from a place of sincerity in order for it to be truly appreciated.

Sincere: You Can Hold Me to It

> So help me God—not even death itself is going to come between us!
>
> —Ruth 1:17, The Message

It doesn't take much to begin marital proceedings. In fact, all that is necessary is a proposal. When the right proposal from the right person in the right place is given, fireworks are released, trumpets sound, and all the wedding strategists fall into formation.

At this point I want to interject this caveat: a proposal can start a marriage, but only a promise can sustain one. My father likes to say, "Once the couple stands at the altar and pronounce, 'I do,' they have the rest of their lives to discover what they did." This is a true statement indeed.

The proposal is an offer that's made (hopefully one that cannot be refused); a promise means we become the offering. In the Old Testament sacrifices were conducted at the altar. And so it is today. Couples stand at the altar to proclaim their devotion to each other as living sacrifices.

When we commit to keeping our promise to our spouse, trust becomes the backbone of our union. The substance of any promise is integrity and fidelity. Integrity denotes truthfulness; fidelity denotes faithfulness. Integrity begins with being true to oneself, and fidelity conveys being honest with others.

Before I proposed to Andrea I made a promise. This promise was not to God, nor was it to Andrea. The promise I made was to me. I promised myself I would be faithful to Andrea in that I would not seduce or become seduced by another woman.

As the Apostle Paul would say, "Bear with me a little in my folly" (2 Cor. 11:1). I strive to be a man of integrity. Thus, there was a time when I had to be true and confront myself. Prior to marrying my wife I was a womanizer. I never knew what it was like to be faithful in one relationship. This is not something that I'm proud of, but it's something I had to overcome.

I prayed to God when I considered proposing to Andrea and asked Him to remove that cheating spirit from my life. I have to say, God did a quick work. When I proposed to Andrea I explained that I couldn't promise how our lives would turn out, but I could promise to be faithful. The basis of my promise was not my love for Andrea, although I love her dearly. The root of my promise was my love for God.

I didn't know much about marriage or what we were getting into at the time, but I did know one thing—*marriage is holy.* This means marriage does not belong to us; it belongs to God. After making this promise to myself, to my wife, and most importantly, to my God, I discovered the following scripture:

> I made a covenant with my eyes not to look with lust upon a girl. I know full well that Almighty God above sends calamity on those who do. He sees everything I do and every step I take.
>
> —Job 31:1–4, TLB

When we make a promise to anyone we are saying, "You can hold me to it." My promise had to do with fidelity; yours could be with gentleness, forgiveness, patience, etc. Outside of God, no one knows you like you know you. Therefore, admit the area in your life where you struggle most and make the promise to overcome it through the power of God.

David and Johnathan had a unique and beautiful relationship. Jonathan was the son of a king; David was the son of a commoner. Although Jonathan outranked David, he saw David as his equal, and to some degree he submitted his life to David.

Jonathan's relationship with David was aggravated and eventually cut short because his father, the king, had a jealous and suspicious spirit toward David. Fearing for his life, David left the kingdom, but before he did he made a promise to his dear friend, Jonathan.

> So Jonathan made a covenant with the family of David, and David swore to it with a terrible curse against himself and his descendants, should he be unfaithful to his promise. But Jonathan made David swear to it

again, this time by his love for him, for he loved him
as much as he loved himself.

—1 SAMUEL 20:16–17, TLB

Unfortunately, David and Jonathan were never given the opportunity to develop the bond they so desired. Jonathan's life was cut short, along with that of his father the king. After David united his kingdom, he fulfilled his promise to Jonathan to treat his family kindly.

David summoned Jonathan's son, restored to him the estate of King Saul (his grandfather), appointed servants to meet his needs, and gave him a place at the royal table (2 Sam. 9:9–13). By this time Jonathan had been deceased for years. Suffice it to say, David made a promise, and he was determined to keep it.

Marriages are made stronger when promises are kept and not taken lightly. The person who keeps their promise is looking for the relationship that is bonding instead of merely binding. To bind anything means "to tie it together on the outside." Consequently, when two people share a bond, they are connected on the inside.

The father in our opening vignette held the hand of his precious daughter. His hand firmly around hers gave assurance of his love and protection. For the sake of trust, support your spouse by holding them up; serve your spouse by not holding back and being sincere to the point they can hold you to what you say. Do this, and see the foundation of your marriage stand firm and secure.

THE LIVING ROOM

We can stand affliction better than we can prosperity,
for in prosperity we forget God.
—Dwight L. Moody

Chapter Two

The Furnace of Affliction

ROLIHLALAH MANDELA WAS born in a small agricultural village in South Africa. As a fairly young child, Mandela attended a mission school, where he acquired the name Nelson. He experienced the death of his father at the tender age of nine, and afterward the tribal king became his guardian.[1]

Mandela eventually relocated to Johannesburg. He took a strong interest in law and attended a university in order to pursue a career in that field. As time progressed, racial injustice, coupled with the fact that many of his black contemporaries were uneducated and impoverished, led him to become an advocate for African rights.

Mandela became the voice and fighting force for a people who had suffered through the wicked system of apartheid. He endured many personal sufferings and finally lost his freedom.

Nelson Mandela paid a heavy price for speaking against apartheid. At the age of forty-four, he was sentenced to life in prison. It would appear Mandela's future was dark and dismal.

Like Nelson Mandela, we all will encounter suffering. No one is exempt from facing trials. Sooner or later trouble is coming our way. However, those marriages that are equipped to face the challenges will remain standing when the smoke clears, and those that are not ready will crumble under the pressure.

Life can be cruel. If marriage is likened to a house, we can't avoid the living room. The living room is where you find the fireplace. Interestingly, in a house there is a place reserved for fire. Even with this knowledge, we enter the house and enjoy many facets it has to offer.

Well, our marriage is the same way. Marriage is not a place we go to escape the issues of life. In marriage we are confronted with physical, emotional, and financial fires, just to name a few. Consequently, we learn to stifle the fires and not allow them to consume us. In some cases, we learn to appreciate the fires because they make us better people.

In the living room of marriage there is a furnace of affliction. If we learn the ABC's of suffering, our union will come through the fire better, having been tried.

ACCEPT SUFFERING

> Dear brothers, is your life full of difficulties and temptations? Then be happy, for when the way is rough, your patience has a chance to grow. So let it grow, and don't try to squirm out of your problems. For when your patience is finally in full bloom, then you will be ready for anything, strong in character, full and complete.
>
> —JAMES 1:2–4, TLB

Let's face it; suffering is a part of life, so we know it comes with the marriage package. Since there's no way of getting around suffering, we just need to accept it. However, let me pause for a moment of clarity. The suffering we need to accept should come from outside elements that the couple can endure together. By no way am I advocating that a person should endure suffering from the hands of a spouse, such as in the case of domestic violence. I have a whole chapter dedicated to this unfortunate subject in my book *Marriage Medicine: Character Is the Cure.*

The Apostle James said that our response to suffering should be joy (James 1:2–3). He reasoned that the suffering (temptations or trials) are there to strengthen our character. It's important for us to understand that the devil presents temptations to bring out the worst in us; God delivers, tests, or tries us to bring out our best.

Marriage will certainly bring out the worst or best in people. Marriage has a living room. In this room we will be tested on the basis of who we really are, not who we think we are. It seems that more than ever before couples are contemplating divorce more than committing to the vows they made to one another.

The Center for Disease Control and Prevention (CDC) has reported that within the past decade the divorce rate has declined.[2] However, before we celebrate that report we must know within the past decade the marriage rate has declined as well. In essence, the attrition in divorces is a direct correlation of people forgoing marriage altogether. The CDC report shows us many don't accept suffering in marriage; they avoid it by not getting married at all.

By choosing the option of avoiding marriage people forfeit the opportunity to test their integrity and fidelity. Remember, integrity is being true to one's self, while fidelity is being true and faithful to the other. Unmarried couples can walk away from each other in extremely difficult times and feel the only offence is to each other.

The couple that chooses marriage should feel more compelled to work it out, because their offence goes even higher. Sure, they vowed to be faithful to each other, but more importantly, their marriage belongs to God.

God created marriage not to make us happy but to make us holy. We have entered into a holy matrimony. This means the union doesn't belong to either spouse, it belongs to God. Now, I'm aware what I just said doesn't come off too appealing. However, it needs to be understood that we must seek God's holiness, which is to say, to live for Him. Now, once we capture God's holiness, the by-product is happiness. Subsequently, we become hopeful, helpful and our marriage is healthy. This is the difference between having *matrimony* and discussing *alimony*.

In the living room of our marriage we must be willing to endure the sufferings. We can do this when we understand the suffering is not a punishment; it's an assignment. God will use our suffering as a testimony to others that He is able to deliver us out of every predicament.

> Many are the afflictions of the righteous: but the LORD delivereth him out of them all.
>
> —PSALM 34:19

The three Hebrew boys were threatened with death by fire by the Babylonian king. The king demanded that the boys bow down to him or be thrown in the furnace (Dan. 3:15). The boys could have cowered at the demands in order to save their lives. They could have avoided the king's punishment; rather, they chose to see it as the Lord's assignment. Read their resolve:

> If it be so, our God whom we serve is able to deliver us from the burning fiery furnace, and he will deliver us out of thine hand, O king. But if not, be it known unto thee, O king, that we will not serve thy gods, nor worship the golden image which thou hast set up.
>
> —DANIEL 3:17–18

Their account should reflect the commitment of all who serve the Lord. As a result of their response, they were placed in the furnace of affliction, but the Bible records the Lord was in the fire with them. Remarkably, in the midst of flames they were walking with the Lord (Dan. 3:25). Interestingly, the Bible doesn't convey the boys saw the Lord; it does say the king saw Him.

If you're married and going through the furnace of affliction, don't quit. Accept the assignment of suffering. Learn to praise the Lord in pain. Allow the joy of the Lord to be your strength. And remember, we must have joy—not instead of the storms or in spite of the storms; we must have joy in the midst of the storms.

When others witness our response in the furnace of affliction, they will see hope for their problems. Even more, they'll see God and not their problems.

Benefit from Suffering

> Every man's work shall be made manifest: for the day shall declare it, because it shall be revealed by fire; and the fire shall try every man's work of what sort it is. If any man's work abide which he hath built thereupon, he shall receive a reward. If any man's work shall be burned, he shall suffer loss: but he himself shall be saved; yet so as by fire.
>
> —1 Corinthians 3:13–15

Once we accept suffering is the inevitable, the next step is to understand we can use suffering to our advantage.

No couple in the Bible endured more suffering than Job and his wife. They suffered the loss of their property, prosperity, and posterity (Job 1:13–19). And this didn't happen in the course of a lifetime; it all took place in one day. On top of this, Job was ostracized in the community, persecuted by his friends and family, and had to endure disease.

In the midst of his trials Job proclaimed:

> But he knoweth the way that I take: when he hath tried me, I shall come forth as gold.
>
> —Job 23:10

We must admit, many of God's children couldn't take the suffering of Job head on and stand after the smoke clears. Too many people fold their marital tent, throw in the matrimony towel, and try to unlock their wedlock for issues more miniscule than what Job faced. This is because we have not faced the fact that suffering is not for our detriment but our benefit.

We might not ever endure all the suffering of Job (who wants to), but we will endure the suffering of problems, pain, and people. And we can do this knowing that God will use the affliction to work for us not against us (Rom. 8:28). One of the greatest principles I've learned for my life is: What life does to us depends on what life finds in us. In other words, the suffering we endure in our marriages and in our lives will reveal who we are, not who we think we are.

The prophet Malachi declared that God is both the refiner's fire and the Refiner (Mal. 3:2–3). His role is to purge all impurities from our lives. The way the refiner determines that the gold is purified is by seeing his image in the metal. So it is with God. He places us in the furnace of affliction not to break us but to make us in His image.

You might say, "I have done a lot of dirt in my life, and it's too much for God to clean up." My friend, God cleans the deepest stain and the most decadent stench. Moreover, only God can use the dirt in our lives and make it work for our good.

A farmer's donkey fell in a pit. The farmer had no means by which to recover the animal, so he figured the donkey would eventually die. As a sign of mercy, the farmer decided to throw dirt in the pit in order to end the animal's suffering.

The animal let out a miserable cry as dirt descended upon him. Suddenly, the donkey had an epiphany. He decided every time the farmer threw dirt on him he would shake the dirt off and step on it. He did this until eventually he was back on level ground.

This is what God wants you to do in your marriage. When life tries to throw the dirt of debt, doubt, divorce, and death on top of you, just shake it off and step on it. Whatever you do, never allow the adversary to have the final word. Realize the dirt the devil attempts to use as your burial plot, God will use for His planting pot.

> I waited patiently for the LORD; and he inclined unto me, and heard my cry. He brought me up also out of an horrible pit, out of the miry clay, and set my feet upon a rock, and established my goings.
>
> —PSALM 40:1–2

COMMIT SUFFERING TO THE LORD

> Let him have all your worries and cares, for he is always thinking about you and watching everything that concerns you.
>
> —1 PETER 5:7, TLB

I counsel couples concerning the sufferings of this world, and I frequently advise them not to worry but to focus on the Lord. Usually the response I receive is an external sigh of agreement. However, just by looking them in the eyes I can sense a thunder of frustration, cloud of confusion, and a tsunami of other emotions simmering internally.

To these people and others like them I make my plea, "Let go and let God." When we face a challenge that is too great for us, all we have to do as a couple is come into agreement in prayer. And after we go to God about how big our problems are, we need to turn around and go to our problems confessing the bigness of our God.

There's no need to live defeated or deflated, not when we have God on our side. God knew we would suffer, and He gave us faith. Faith is not to save us from the furnace of affliction; it is to settle us while in the furnace of affliction.

Jesus comforted us with these words:

> I have told you all this so that you will have peace of
> heart and mind. Here on earth you will have many
> trials and sorrows; but cheer up, for I have overcome
> the world.
>
> —JOHN 16:33, TLB

Elkanah and Hannah were facing a tough time. They loved
one another dearly and deeply. This fact was not enough to
grant them what they desired most—a child.

As was the custom, Elkanah had another wife. His second
wife was named Peninnah, and she had children with
Elkanah in abundance. Peninnah made life for Hannah
unbearable. She relentlessly ridiculed Hannah for not having
children. As a result of the harsh treatment, Hannah spent
many days weeping and fasting.

It pained Elkanah to see his beloved Hannah grieving
this way. Now, he could have gotten bent out of shape with
the troublesome wife. He could have blamed God for not
allowing Hannah to bear children. Rather than worry, he
chose to worship. The Bible reveals in the midst of all the
mess Elkanah continued to go to the house of God (1 Sam.
1:3).

As Elkanah and Hannah chose to praise the Lord in the
midst of their pain, God opened Hannah's womb. The couple
named their son Samuel and raised him to follow and revere
God. Samuel would later become the last judge of Israel and
would be instrumental in the transition from King Saul
(Israel's first king) to King David (Israel's beloved king).

When we commit our suffering to the Lord He gives us
assurance for our anxieties, power for the pain, and faith
for our fears. We ought not to follow the Lord blindly; we
should follow Him boldly, knowing our afflictions are for a
moment to make us better along the way.

After decades of imprisonment Nelson Mandela was finally
released. One would think that after the brutalities suffered

he would be bitter. However, he allowed his afflictions to make him a better man. Some thought if released Mandela would seek reprisal, but he chose the path of reconciliation.[3]

Out of the shadows of South Africa's apartheid emerged this man, a historical figure, to defend against racial injustice. Mandela campaigned and eventually became South Africa's first black president. In essence, he made it through the furnace of affliction.

The strategy for every struggle is to utilize the ABC's of suffering. Learn to celebrate, not just tolerate, suffering. And the next time you receive persecution, remember: promotion is on the horizon.

THE DINING ROOM

Be thankful for what you have; you'll end up having more. If you concentrate on what you don't have, you will never, ever have enough.

—OPRAH WINFREY

Chapter Three

Count Your Blessings

I CAN RECALL ONE of my professors in college giving the entire class a self-evaluation. He challenged each student to define who they were in one word.

The challenge captivated my attention. The professor proceeded to instruct the class, but I was stuck pondering his puzzle. How could I define who I am in one word? Surely, the complexities of my life deserve more than just one word.

Soon the class had concluded, but that conundrum lingered on with me. As I pulled into my driveway I couldn't help noticing two plaques I had mounted on the two pillars at the entryway. One plaque read *Carpe* and the other *Diem*. This is a Latin term that means "seize the day."

As I approached my front door I saw my customized address plaque that read, "Love lives here!" Once inside the house I proceeded to greet my lovely daughters and kiss my beautiful wife. A couple of hours later we gathered in the dining room to partake of the evening's meal. At the table we discussed the adventures the day had presented for us all.

As the evening came to a close, the ruckus in the house was replaced with silence. Once my daughters were sound asleep in their beds and my wife was out like a light, I decided it was time for me to do the same.

Just when my head hit the pillow, the answer to the professor's challenge hit me. If I could define the totality of my personality in one word, if I needed a word to comprise my past, present, and future, that word would be *thankful*.

The reason for my gratitude is God's goodness.

When we enter the dining room of our marriage we must be mindful to be thankful. In the dining room we are provided sustenance to satisfy our hunger. However, the dining room is not a place for greedy hands but rather grateful hearts.

Jesus was hungry (Matt. 4:1–3). In His famished hour the devil appeared to tempt Him to distrust God. The devil snarled, "If thou be the Son of God, command that these stones be made bread" (v. 3).

Spiritually speaking, stones represent hard times and bread represents pleasure, fulfillment for our appetite. In essence, the devil was insinuating that a child of God shouldn't have to endure tough times. Jesus' response was simple and yet profound. He replied, "Man shall not live by bread alone, but by every word that proceedeth out of the mouth of God."

No matter who you are or where you are, if you're serving God, the devil will always tell you to live without the stones (hard times). However, as people of God we know rocks are needed to build a faith-filled, fortified house. Rocks are especially needed to build a marriage. Therefore, in the dining room, we learn to count our blessings with the rocks.

Water Out of the Rock

> And gavest them bread from heaven for their hunger, and broughtest forth water for them out of the rock for their thirst...
>
> —Nehemiah 9:15

Every couple needs to know there are always more blessings than there are problems. The rocks in our marriage may represent the problems we could have with wayward children. It could represent the ever-increasing bills in the mailbox. Maybe someone's rock is them having to cope with sickness. Whatever rock we may have to face, God is able to bring water out of it.

The water represents *spiritual blessings.* In the Bible water is a picture of God's Word (John 15:3; Eph. 5:26). Many marriages are burdened with problem after problem and sorrow upon sorrow because the Word of God does not take precedence in the union.

In order for your marriage to remain strong the Word of God must take center stage. Without God's theology we are left with our own philosophy. Our marriage will not flourish based upon what we think or how we feel, because sooner or later we won't see eye to eye with our spouse. When this occurs the question becomes, Who's right? The answer is always emphatically, God.

When the difficulties of life visit our homes, the devil appears with, "If you are the child of God, command the stones to be removed." This is when we must pray! Note: We should never pray for fewer problems; we must pray for more power. Afterward, we need to get in God's Word, because that is where the answers to life's problems are found.

A teenage girl by the name of Mary was told she would be given God's greatest gift to carry for the sake of the world (Luke 1:27–33). Now, this was more news than any young girl could handle. Perplexed, Mary inquired how she would be able to carry this great burden without a man's help.

After an angel rehearsed God's providential plan Mary was still confused. Yet, she did not allow her bewilderment to botch the plan of God for her life. By faith, Mary declared, "Be it unto me according to thy word" (v. 38).

When couples learn to handle hardness the way Mary did according to the Word of God, their marriages will receive strength. Rocks can either become obstacles or opportunities, stumbling blocks or stepping stones. If we doubt God, we'll only see rocks. When we trust Him, He'll provide water—His promise of victory, not defeat.

Jesus gave an example of two men: one wise, the other foolish. He said both men were building their house, and both houses were tested by hardship. The wise man's house stood tall after the test, whereas the foolish man's house succumbed to the pressure (Matt. 7:24–27).

The question becomes, Why did one stand and the other fall? Well, the deciding factor was the wise man's appreciation and application of the Word of God. The foolish man did not use God's Word while building his house, and he paid greatly for that decision. The wise man's house was built on a rock (Matt. 7:24–25). God wants your marriage on the Rock!

Realize the devil uses rocks for your destruction, while God uses them for your construction. God has given us the spiritual blessing of His Word, and we must use it for our spiritual development.

Honey Out of the Rock

> But I would give you the finest wheat and fill you with honey from the rocks.
>
> —Psalm 81:16, NCV

God told Moses He was taking His people to a land flowing with milk and honey (Exod. 3:8). Today God is still fulfilling that promise. Some may say, "I can do without the milk and honey." If this is you, before turning down God's proposition, get a fuller understanding of what He is saying. The milk represents our necessities, and the honey is a picture of our luxuries.

When God said He'll give us honey out of the rock, He was conveying *material blessings*. Make no mistake about it; God wants to see us doing well. He wants us to enjoy life and not endure it. While we certainly need His spiritual blessings, He desires to give us material blessings also. Where you live, the car you drive, the job you have are all material blessings from the Lord. When times are hard and the economic well is all dried up, God wants you to know that He has honey.

In the dining room of our marriage all vegetables and no

deserts can be depressing. No matter what, remember there are always more blessings than problems.

I recall the third year of my marriage. Andrea and I believed God and stepped out by faith. We moved from an apartment and bought our first house.

I remember hearing God say He was doing a new thing with us and that He didn't want to put new wine in old bottles (Matt. 9:17). Call me crazy, but I took that to mean give away the bulk of our furniture and move into the new house. The only furniture we took with us were the bedroom sets. Now, this was not easy, because we had nice stuff, and at the time we didn't have the money to purchase anything new.

One evening while enjoying a Monday night football game in my new house, a thought flashed in my mind. The thought was about Andrea and me receiving new furniture from a particular person. Immediately I repented because I figured the thought came from me. I didn't like the idea of picturing someone buying us stuff because I wanted us to work, save, and buy our furniture ourselves.

The following evening Andrea was extremely late getting home. I begin to worry because that was uncharacteristic of her. Finally, she called me and was very excited on the other end of the phone. When I inquired about her enthusiasm, she told me that she was at the furniture store, and ironically, with the person who popped in my head the night before.

She went on to say God had instructed that person to buy our living room set. Needless to say, I was speechless and in utter shock because the Lord showed me what He would do and who He would use to do it. From that time to now, Andrea and I have learned to count our blessings.

We had no money to purchase furniture. I guess you could say we were stuck between a rock and a hard place. (I had to go there.) Nevertheless, God can bring honey out of a rock. The material blessings didn't stop there, but I'll save them for another time or another book. I'm sure when you take time to think you can remember when God brought honey out of your rock, when He made a way for you and your family when there wasn't a way.

The devil doesn't want you to receive God's honey. He's hoping you cannot recall God's honey in your life, but so what! Never give the devil final authority. For every rock that Satan brings in your life, God provides honey.

> My child, eat honey because it is good. Honey from the honeycomb tastes sweet.
>
> —PROVERBS 24:13, NCV

Now, I must submit this admonishment: God wants us to have possessions, but He doesn't want the possessions to have us. Therefore, we must be wise not to get caught up with going after things. Marriages suffer when this happens.

Never misappropriate love. We are to love people and use things. However, the philosophy of the world is to use people and love things. If we go down that path, eventually we'll use people to get the things we love. The Bible notes, "For the love of money is the root of all evil" (1 Tim. 6:10). Money itself is not evil. To covet after money is evil.

God wants us to have money. The Scripture reveals money answers all things (Eccles. 10:19). However, the Lord doesn't want money to be the motivation of our hearts.

If we focus more on the blessing than the Giver of the blessing we are guilty of idolatry. If we complain about the blessings we are guilty of ingratitude. If we hoard the blessings and do not share them with others we are guilty of indulgence. If we count our blessings with a sincere heart of gratitude, God will bestow more on us.

> The blessing of the LORD, it maketh rich, and he addeth no sorrow with it.
>
> —PROVERBS 10:22

The next time the devil confronts your marriage with his rocks, consider that the Lord has honey; then taste and see that the Lord is good (Ps. 34:8).

ROLL AWAY THE ROCK

"Roll the stone aside," Jesus told them.
—JOHN 11:39, TLB

A university football team had suffered the worse losing season in the program's history. Not wanting to repeat that horrific season the following year, the coach sent a scout searching for an outstanding athlete.

The scout enquired earnestly, "What kind of athlete are you looking for?" The coach, while clinching his fist, replied, "Well, you know there's that guy who gets knocked down and just stays down?" The scout knew the coach couldn't possibly want that kind of guy, so he asked, "We don't want him, do we?" The coach quickly responded, "No, we don't want him!" And with veins bulging from his forehead the coach stated, "Then there's that guy who gets knocked down and gets up and then gets knocked down again and stays down."

The scout inquired, "We don't want him either, do we?" The coach concurred, "No! Leave him where you found him." Now with his jawbones tightening, the coach exclaimed, "In your search you might find the guy who gets knocked down, gets back up, gets knocked down again and gets back up again and again." The scout enthusiastically probed, "That's the guy we want, right?" Then the coach yelled, "No, we don't want him either. I want you to find that guy who's knocking everybody down—that's the guy we want!"

My friend, the Lord doesn't want you to take the devil's attack lying down. Therefore, He has empowered you to roll away the rocks. The ability to roll away the rocks or to handle life's hardships is God's *physical blessing*.

You might be a person that is up in years. If so, it doesn't matter. Caleb was promised his piece of land from the Lord in his early years. This man walked with God and went to war for God. I'm sure there were many days when he was tired; however, he never threw in the towel.

Caleb was given the promise to receive land at the age of forty. He didn't actually possess his parcel of land until he was eighty-five. Wow! This was a man who knew how to get a hold of the promises of God and not let go. Read this valiant man of faith's testimony for yourself:

> As yet I am as strong this day as I was in the day that Moses sent me: as my strength was then, even so is my strength now, for war, both to go out, and to come in. Now therefore give me this mountain, whereof the LORD spake in that day.
>
> —JOSHUA 14:11–12

I hope you can sense my excitement. Somehow my back gets a little straighter and my strength is renewed just thinking about this powerful patriarch of the faith.

In case you missed it, Caleb asked for his mountain. A mountain is a massive rock. Caleb didn't shrink in the day of adversity; he wasn't moved by life's challenges. He took hold of the promise of God, and he rode that promise through the passage of pain. In the end, Caleb received his piece of the rock. He and his children were blessed by God.

Beloved, don't allow your marriage to suffer because you won't believe God's promise. Don't refuse the Lord's blessing; rather use the Lord's physical blessing to obtain what's yours.

God instructed Joshua to command the leaders of Israel to retrieve twelve stones from the Jordan River. They were to carry the stones from the river and place them as a memorial to represent that a mighty God can empower a feeble people (Josh. 4:1–7). He is able to bring water out of the rock, honey from the rock and He can empower us to roll away the rock.

Just about every night when I arrive home, I reflect on the various challenges of the day. I kiss my wife and daughters. No matter what rocks may be in store for us, I lay my head on my pillow in peace. For I know as long as I continue to count my blessings, I can count on my God.

As long as you count the God-given spiritual, material, and physical blessings, you may count on Him as well. Above all, if you ever hit rock bottom, see it as a sure foundation and a new beginning knowing the only direction is up.

THE KITCHEN

The meaning of life. The wasted years of life. The poor choices of life. God answers the mess of life with one word: grace.

—Max Lucado

Chapter Four

A Message in the Mess

A DAUGHTER COMPLAINED TO her father about life's difficulties. She explained how nothing had been going her way and how trouble seemed to know her address.

Her father, who happened to be a top chef, took her to the kitchen. He filled three pots with water and placed them on separate fires so that they began to boil. In one he placed carrots, in another he placed eggs, and in the last pot he poured coffee beans. Silently, he let them boil in the water.

Minutes later the father turned off the burners. He removed the carrots, eggs and coffee from their perspective pots and placed them each in their own bowl. Turning to his frantic daughter he asked, "Darling, what do you see?" "Carrots, eggs and coffee," she replied.

Sensing his message was not sinking in, he asked her to feel the carrots. She did; they were soft. He then asked her to break one of the eggs. After removing the shell, she held the hard-boiled egg. Last, he instructed her to take a drink of the coffee. She smiled as she tasted its deep flavor. She humbly asked, "Daddy, what does all this mean?"

The sage old chef explained each item was subjected to the same pressure, boiling water. However, each responded differently to the stimulus. The carrot went in strong and stiff, but after being submerged in the boiling water, it weakened. The egg with its thin shell had been fragile, but the boiling water caused the egg to harden. The coffee beans were unique. After making contact with the boiling water, they changed the water.

He asked his daughter, "Which are you?"

As we visit the kitchen of our marriage, we must prepare ourselves for the mess. The kitchen is where cooking takes place. Normally, children are not allowed in the kitchen because adults are busy creating cuisines, and playing is not preferred.

People who desire marriage must be cautioned that the marital union comes equipped with a kitchen. Therefore, it takes maturity from the husband and wife if the union is to flow in unity. When immature people get married, selfishness is at the head of the table. Furthermore, juvenile individuals seek self-gratification, and the marriage suffers as a result.

Marriages that are occupied by mature, selfless folks are built to last because each looks to help the other when times get messy. It's true, the kitchen can get messy, but no need for alarm, because there's a message in the mess.

THE MESS OF BAGGAGE: THE WEIGHT

> Let us strip off every weight that slows us down, especially the sin that so easily trips us up.
>
> —HEBREWS 12:1, NLT

Whenever I fly anywhere I do my best to pack for the occasion. In warm or cold climate, I pack accordingly. If I'm going to be preaching in a church I bring a suit; if I'm teaching a marriage seminar I tend to dress casually. Wherever I'm going, my goal is to have one piece of luggage.

Andrea is a different story. It doesn't matter where she is going or how long she is staying, she packs half her closet. Her suitcase is usually replete with shoes, belts, toiletry items, pants, more shoes, blouses, socks, hosiery, jackets, even more shoes, plastic bags for soiled laundry, snacks, and did I mention shoes, sleepwear, summer wear, winter wear, formal wear, and just in case she loses a pair, more shoes. Sufficient to say, by the time Andrea's finished packing she has more baggage than an Olympic team traveling overseas. I mean really, she ought to be sponsored by Louis Vuitton.

And would you believe she has the nerve to ask me if there is room in my bag for her additional items.

I love my wife dearly, but a simple trip to her becomes a major expedition. I've tried explaining the importance of traveling light. (It didn't work.) I've tried getting her therapy, counseling, and even a certified hypnotist. (Of course, I'm kidding.) Bottom line: I've come to accept that traveling with my wife means carrying a lot of baggage.

Every time we travel, Andrea promises she'll do better, and because I love her, I'm patient. You may ask, "Tyrone, why all the fuss about Andrea's baggage?" The reason for the protest is I'm always left carrying most of it.

This is the reality for many marriages. Couples must be willing to carry each other's baggage. This does not negate the fact that we must reduce the baggage.

Baggage in any relationship is a weight. If we carry them too long they will wear us out and pull us down. However, we can't throw the baby out with the bathwater. We must be patient with our spouse while they look to cope with their issues.

The etymology of the word *baggage* derives from the French word *bagasse*. This word means "worthless, trashy or rubbish."[1]

Too often, people come into marriage with emotional baggage. They are carrying the weight that someone in their past has left. It could be offences committed in previous marriages. It may be the lack of affection from a parent or caretaker in the person's impressionable years.

Our spouse's emotional baggage can get messy, but marriage comes equipped with a kitchen. We learn to excuse the mess in the kitchen because we understand that cooking is underway.

If a person is ever going to rid themselves of emotional baggage, they must own it and not assign it. In other words, they must take responsibility for how they feel and not blame others for how they feel.

The following is a matrix that differentiates between owning and assigning our emotions:

The Emotion	Assigning	Owning
Anger	You make me angry!	I need not get angry so easily.
Depression	You make me depressed!	There's no need to be depressed.
Worry	I worry because of you.	Worrying is a sin. I will trust the Lord.
Regret	I would be better off, but you…	I own my mistakes and look ahead.

The above was just a few of many bad emotions that can affect our marriages in a negative way. We must accept the truth. Another person cannot make us do anything. Their actions can stimulate a response from us, but ultimately every individual has a choice in the matter. Eventually, if we do not get rid of our baggage, we will miss what God wants to do in our lives.

God was setting the stage for Israel's first king to be selected. The Lord began by choosing the tribe, then the family out of the tribe, and finally the man from the family. The man selected as Israel's first king was Saul; however, there was a problem in his coronation. Saul was nowhere to be found.

> Samuel went back to God: "Is he anywhere around?" God said, "Yes, he's right over there—hidden in that pile of baggage." They ran and got him. He took his place before everyone, standing tall—head and shoulders above them. Samuel then addressed the people,

"Take a good look at whom God has chosen: the best!
No one like him in the whole country!"
—1 SAMUEL 10:22–24, THE MESSAGE

Saul came very close to missing his assignment because he was hiding in the baggage. If your spouse is hiding in the baggage, pray for them. Then wait for God to reveal to you how to help them recover.

THE MESS OF BONDAGE: THE WALL

After Jesus said this, he cried out in a loud voice, "Lazarus, come out!" The dead man came out, his hands and feet wrapped with pieces of cloth, and a cloth around his face. Jesus said to them, "Take the cloth off of him and let him go."
—JOHN 11:43–44, NCV

Newlyweds had checked into the honeymoon suite in a classy hotel. It was close to midnight, and they were extremely fatigued from all the celebration.

When they arrived at the suite they were stunned to discover only a sofa and a coffee table with a lamp. Imagine their disappointment—a honeymoon suite with no bed.

While investigating further the couple discovered the sofa was a hide-away-bed equipped with a lumpy mattress and worn-out pillows. Too tired to address the honeymoon suite horror, the couple decided to go ahead and rough it.

The next morning, they both awoke with sore backs. As they checked out of the hotel the husband demanded to speak with management and gave a sour report about the honeymoon suite. Surprised to hear they slept on the sofa, the manager asked, "Why did you sleep in the sitting area?"

The manager then escorted the couple back to the suite and opened a door they assumed a closet. They entered a luxurious room garnished with all the modern amenities and a bed fit for royalty.

Many couples are like the one mentioned in the previous anecdote. They have been given an opportunity to advance in their marriage. The only thing that separated the newlyweds from luxury was a wall. This proverbial wall keeps many couples from moving forward and enjoying their union. They grind and gripe that life has somehow dealt them a bad hand.

Jesus said He came to give us abounding life. In contrast, the devil looks to bind us with all kinds of limitations. The devil presents temptations to bring about the worst possible scenario for us.

The greatest wall the devil can use against us is our pride. Pride keeps us in bondage. It communicates to your spouse, "My way or no way at all." The problem with our way is the road is unfinished. The Bible expresses there is a way that seems right to a man, but it only leads to a dead end (Prov. 16:25).

Some people have placed limitations on their marriage because they have spoken words of bitterness and discouragement to their spouse. In the heat of a verbal disagreement something was said with intentions to hurt. Now, the wheels of progress in their marriage have come to a grinding halt.

The spirit of this is spawn from the devil himself. He is the author of confusion and the father of lies. Satan doesn't care if you're married; he just doesn't want you happily married.

Moses went to the Pharaoh in Egypt and told him to let God's people go and worship the Lord in the wilderness. The Pharaoh's response was that they could go and worship their God, only they couldn't go too far (Exod. 8:28).

Satan is still trying to place limitations on God's people today. He'll tell you that your marriage won't make it; he'll look to convince you that it's no use trying anymore. However, Jesus declared that He came to bring life where you have limitations and to those things that have you bound. He commands them to be loosed and let you go!

> For ye have not received the spirit of bondage again to fear; but ye have received the Spirit of adoption, whereby we cry, Abba, Father.
> —ROMANS 8:15

For some, the bondage ends immediately. For others, it may take some time for it to manifest in the natural. Even still, remain encouraged, knowing that God is working on your behalf.

If you were one of the people who have offended your spouse with your actions or words, go and repair the damage. Start by admitting you were wrong for not allowing the Christ in you to come out. In the kitchen of marriage, cleaning up is inevitable, and you can't be too prideful to get your hands dirty.

Do this and see the places of bondage in your marriage completely broken.

THE MESS OF BANDAGE: THE WOUND

> My wounds stink and are corrupt because of my foolishness. I am troubled; I am bowed down greatly; I go mourning all the day long. For my loins are filled with a loathsome disease: and there is no soundness in my flesh. I am feeble and sore broken: I have roared by reason of the disquietness of my heart. Lord, all my desire is before thee; and my groaning is not hid from thee. My heart panteth, my strength faileth me: as for the light of mine eyes, it also is gone from me. My lovers and my friends stand aloof from my sore; and my kinsmen stand afar off.
> —PSALM 38:5–11

There will invariably come a time when we will get hurt, our spouse will get hurt, and in some cases we hurt one another. When this occurs, we must do what we can to heal the hurts and move forward.

It's very important to remain optimistic in life. Positive people have a way of moving forward no matter what happens. If you are a positive person but you happen to be married to a person not so enthusiastic, don't panic. Just do your best to be there for your mate. Some people need more pick-me-ups than others.

> When my spirit grows faint within me, it is you who watch over my way. In the path where I walk people have hidden a snare for me. Look and see, there is no one at my right hand; no one is concerned for me. I have no refuge; no one cares for my life.
>
> —PSALM 142:3–4, NIV

People who always wear bandages can be messy. These are the people who feel no one loves them or everyone is out to get them. These individuals have a hypochondriac mentality. To those individuals I say weeping may endure for a night, but joy comes in the morning (Ps. 30:5). In other words, don't allow the devil to rain on your parade too long.

> When Jesus saw him and knew how long he had been ill, he asked him, "Would you like to get well?" "I can't," the sick man said, "for I have no one to help me into the pool at the movement of the water. While I am trying to get there, someone else always gets in ahead of me." Jesus told him, "Stand up, roll up your sleeping mat and go on home!"
>
> —JOHN 5:6–8, TLB

Even if you are physically ill, there's no need to be spiritually sick. I personally know of people who have been battling with all kinds of diseases, such as diabetes, lupus, sarcoidosis, cancer, and the list goes on; you wouldn't know these people were inflicted unless someone told you, because although they are wounded they do not wear the wounds. More than a few of them have told me that they will not allow the disease to steal their joy. The disease may have altered their lives, but it has not controlled their lives.

Unlike the man Jesus spoke to at the pool, in marriage we have someone there to help us get up when we're down. However, if for some reason your spouse is not there, the Lord is there to remove the wounds and empower you to stand.

Jesus commanded the sick man to stand up, take up his bed, and go home. In essence, Jesus was saying, "The issue that once held you, you now hold it." That man's wound was his bed. Your wounds, whatever they may be, can be removed if you look to Jesus.

For those of us who focus on the Lord, the sun never sets; for those that fail to focus on the Lord, the sun never rises. Even when the day is dark and the clouds are thick, we must remember that the sun is shining. It may be behind the clouds, but sooner or later the sun's rays will penetrate the darkness.

It's not healthy to always keep bandages on a wound. At some point they must be removed. Some people like to wear bandages like a badge. They want other people to know they were hurt.

> And all his sons and all his daughters rose up to comfort him; but he refused to be comforted; and he said, For I will go down into the grave unto my son mourning. Thus his father wept for him.
>
> —Genesis 37:35

There are times in our lives when we need to grieve; it's healthy for us to do so. However, at some point we must remove the grave clothes, refuse to be the victim, and in Christ, stand as the victor.

When we're married we must do our best to help one another remove the bandages, push each other beyond the bondage, and help carry the baggage.

In the opening tale, the daughter was left to make a decision. She pondered whether to be the carrot that softens in trouble, the egg that hardens in difficulties, or the coffee bean that changes its environment. Fortunately, she chose to become like the coffee bean. The father took time to hear his daughter's pain. Nevertheless, he seized the moment to teach her a very valuable lesson. What life does to us depends on what life finds in us.

We too have a Father who cares how we handle the mess in our lives. Like the daughter, we have a choice. We can turn tragedy to triumph, adversity to advantage; we can choose to be a victor, not a victim.

Life can be messy. Marriage can be messy. But there's a message in the mess. The message is maturity. Become mature in the midst of it all and allow God to get the glory. When that happens, others will receive the gain, we'll obtain the growth, and it will all work out for the good.

THE HALLWAY

Love is our true destiny. We do not find the meaning of
life by ourselves alone—we find it with another.
—Thomas Merton

twOne

B Y MAY 1937, one of America's most famous landmarks was ready for use. At this time the Golden Gate Bridge, the world's longest suspension bridge, boasted a 4,200-foot-long suspension span. It is estimated billions of vehicles have crossed the colossal passage since opening to the public.[1]

Dating back to 1849, after the Gold Rush, opportunists looking to capitalize concluded connecting the northern part of the city of San Francisco to Marin County, California, with a bridge would bring the community a mass fortune. Prior to this endeavor, the only way to travel between these two areas was by ferry.

Joseph B. Strauss was the bridge's chief engineer. Both he and those who took on the monumental task of constructing the bridge faced opposition from many skeptics. Among the doubters were city officials whose only concern was the financial weight the project would place on the cities. Then there were ferry operators who feared access to the bridge would cause a decline in business revenues. Strauss's contemporaries in the engineering community declared the whole notion of the bridge technically impossible to construct.

It seemed even nature played against the bridge's construction crew, as they had to contend with strong ocean currents, heavy winds, and fog in the Golden Gate Strait. On February 17, 1937, it was tragically recorded that ten workers died as a result of equipment malfunction. Altogether, eleven men died during the construction of the bridge.

In spite of these issues, the Golden Gate Bridge was completed in four years. Nearly a quarter of a million spectators witnessed its opening on May 27, 1937.

So far, we've been looking at the importance of various rooms in a house and how they correlate to areas in our marriage. One area in the house that is often overlooked but is crucial to the house's structure is the hallway.

Connecting the northern and southern parts of the Bay area was critical economically and socially. The same can be said concerning the connection of the husband and wife. Just as the Bridge connected the Bay, the hallway connects the rooms, and there must be a connection between the husband and wife.

Jesus was challenged on the issue of divorce. The Pharisees asked, "Can a man divorce his wife for every cause?" Jesus responded by simply saying nothing should come between the partners (Matt. 19:3–6).

Jesus quoted the Father by saying the two should become one. The concept of two becoming one has inspired the term *twOne*. This of course, is the numbers two and one coming together, and where they meet is at the zero. In other words, if the concept of two becoming one is to prevail, if there is a genuine connection, nothing must come between them.

Consider the point of zero in the word *twOne* as the hallway in your house. For there to be easy passage we must clear, close, and clean any obstructions in the hallway of the marriage. No matter how you slice it, the obstructions that could stifle a couple's connection are people, places, and things.

WE MUST CLEAR PEOPLE

> Look around. Isn't there plenty of land out there? Let's separate. If you go left, I'll go right; if you go right, I'll go left.
> —GENESIS 13:9, THE MESSAGE

People are great to have around. After all, there is strength in numbers. I love people. I love the stimuli of good conversation, the excitement of positive interaction, and even the thrill of constructive competition.

Albeit, with all my enthusiasm for people, I understand there are times reserved for just my wife and I. I'm willing to bet the person who initially said, "Two's company; three's a crowd," was either married or discovered that axiom from someone who was married.

It troubles me to see marriages stressed to the point of divorce because one of the partners would rather spend more time with those outside the union. Yes, it's good to have friends but not to the point of damaging your marriage. Some people can't let go of past relationships. Have you ever stopped to think there's a reason the relationship is in the past? So let it pass.

We're living in the Facebook era, and more and more I'm seeing marriages destroyed because one of the partners is adamant about keeping up with their friends. The truth of the matter is that most of the chatter on Facebook is gossip and sending out photos. I've maintained the position "to each his own," but I do say, be careful about whom you're calling friends.

I tend to believe oftentimes when spouses dispute over the other's friend, the person being discussed isn't a friend at all. Too often there is an illicit relationship happening, and the spouse refuses to admit it. If this is the case, let it go and seek spiritual counseling because it's not worth disappointing your family and disrespecting your God.

God wanted to have a personal relationship with Abraham; therefore, He instructed Abraham to clear his calendar and clear some people (Gen. 12:1). Abraham informed his wife Sarah of the Lord's instructions, but he didn't comply totally. Abraham departed from his kinfolk like the Lord had told him to do, but there was one problem. He took his nephew Lot with him.

Now, Abraham was a man of worship, and he would commune with God on a daily basis. On the other hand, Lot had no fellowship with God, but he profited from his uncle's relationship with the Lord. The Bible says both men came into great wealth to the degree that the land couldn't hold all their possessions. Also, great tension rose between Abraham and Lot's herdsmen.

Realizing his error in not totally obeying God, Abraham

suggested he and Lot separate (Gen. 13:8–9). There comes a time when we must clear people out of our lives because they're not a part of the picture God has for our future. This was the case for Abraham.

Abraham could have reasoned, I have plenty and Lot has plenty; therefore, we need to remain together. This is the mistake many make. They remain in ungodly relationships because of what the other person brings to the table. Abraham didn't need Lot as long as He had God. And you don't need a "Lot," as long as you put God first in your life.

This would not be the first time Abraham would have to learn the lesson of clearing people. Years later while Sarah was weaning their baby son Isaac, she was mocked by Abraham's eldest son. Sarah demanded that Abraham put the child and his mother Hagar out of their house.

The situation grieved Abraham. He didn't want to see his eldest child abandoned. God spoke to His friend Abraham and confirmed he would have to obey his wife's request (Gen. 21:12). God also promised to provide for his eldest son.

The point here was for Abraham to save his marriage by clearing the people who got between him and his wife. If it's time to clear the hallway of your marriage by clearing some people. Wait no longer. Do it and see your marriage progress to the next level of love and satisfaction.

WE MUST CLOSE PLACES

> Elisha, the man of God, sent a message to the king of Israel, saying, "Be careful! Don't pass that place, because the Arameans are going down there!"
> —2 KINGS 6:9, NCV

There are places that can do more harm than good, and we must be aware of them before it's too late. It used to be when a person wanted to escape they had to leave the house. This is no longer the case. With the advent of the Internet a person can leave reality and become whoever they desire without leaving their home.

It's sad, but we see it all the time. People are on the Internet creating all kinds of havoc. There's a new phenomenon called cyberbullying. This is when unruly young people are threatening other youngsters. Unfortunately, there are reported cases where the victims of the bullying have committed suicide.

The Internet is a great tool in the hands of responsible people; however, it's a dangerous toy in those not so responsible. It's a place where you can connect with total strangers and plan secret rendezvous. It's a place where pornographic material is popularized and publicized every waking moment.

In short, the Internet is known as the Web. This term is true in every sense of the word. Like a spider that entraps its prey with the web it spins, the Internet can capture its users and claim their time, money, and eventually their lives. Some can stay isolated on the Web for days like a bear in a cave.

> There Elijah went into a cave and stayed all night. Then the LORD spoke his word to him: "Elijah! Why are you here?"
> —1 KINGS 19:9, NCV

Elijah found himself in a place that distracted him from his mission. His cave represented a mental place where he had withdrawn.

Some people withdraw in bars or nightclubs; others find themselves joining groups or programs just to keep from going home. If you are in a place that has interfered with the connection between you and your spouse, the Lord is saying, "Come away from there." A lot of women find shopping as an outlet or alternative to dealing with the issues at home. The stores are called an outlet for a reason. Beware: You might choose the outlet and regret the outcome!

The Scriptures tell of a time when there was a famine in Bethlehem. One particular man by the name of Elimelech decided to avoid the famine by leaving his native land and seeking better accommodations. He took his wife and two sons with him. They decided to settle down in a country called Moab (Ruth 1:1–5).

Ironically, Elimelech and his two sons died in Moab. They left the place of God—trying to avoid death—only to meet death where they chose to reside. Word got back to Elimelech's wife, Naomi, that all was well in the home country. She went back home and discovered God took care of everyone. In essence, their outlet didn't provide the expected outcome.

Don't leave home because there's pressure. Keep the hallways of your marriage free of disturbance by closing the door to any distractions. Don't place unnecessary stress on your family. Close the places that need to be closed, and stay in the place where you have God's protection and grace. Remember, the will of God will never lead you where the grace of God cannot keep you.

WE MUST CLEAN THINGS

> So don't sit around on your hands! No more dragging your feet! Clear the path for long-distance runners so no one will trip and fall, so no one will step in a hole and sprain an ankle. Help each other out.
> —HEBREWS 12:13, THE MESSAGE

Growing up in my house as a young boy one thing was a certainty: you learned to clean up after yourself. My mother had to raise three boys, and I will admit we were a handful. Saturday was the designated day to clean the entire apartment. Albeit, the place that had to remain clean throughout the week was the hallway.

Even now, I can hear my mother's commanding voice telling me to remove my toys from the hallway. She would say, "Keep my hallway clean from stuff so people can pass through freely!" One night, I heard my mother's voice scream out in pain in the dark. While on her way to the bathroom, she stepped on my toy racecar. Needless to say, I got reprimanded.

Today many couples are stumbling and steering their way through stuff left in the hallway of their marriages. Again, when I speak of the hallway of marriage, I'm referring to how they connect with one another. Nothing cleans the hallway of marriage better than communication.

One day a couple sought marital counseling. The counselor asked, "What seems to be the problem?" The couple sat quietly for a moment when the wife finally complained, "We need to communicate." Stunned, the husband countered, "What do you mean we don't communicate? Just yesterday I texted a reply to the message you left me on Facebook."

Mark it down; when the communication stops in a marriage, the union is on its way to a funeral. The tombstone will read "Here lies a marriage once alive with love and peace, soon found with rigor mortis, for communication has finally ceased."

The following matrix[2] shows the five talks that will build a strong marriage and keep a strong connection in the union:

Five Talks of Communication in Marriage	
Silly Talk	These are the moments you take to make each other laugh and humorous accounts that occur during the day that you share with one another.
Significant Talk	These are heart-to-heart talks. These are times when you share your inner feelings with each other.
Self-Talk	This is self-motivation in order to keep a positive attitude. This is also reminding yourself you are loved.

Five Talks of Communication in Marriage	
Spiritual Talk	In these discussions you encourage one another with the Word of God. This can also include times for Bible study together.
Sweet Talk	These are times when you say really nice things to each other. You could refer to one another with pet names or mentioning your physical attraction toward each other.

The couple in the Bible who experienced a disconnect due to lack of communication is Isaac and Rebecca. Theirs is a love story right out of romance novels. He was quiet and calm; she was beautiful and adventurous. Rebecca was brought to meet Isaac from a distant land. When the two met it was truly love at first sight. They were inseparable. The Bible records that Isaac could be found *sporting* his wife (Gen. 26:8). Now, courting and sporting are two different levels of communication. You can court someone privately. However, to sport someone is open and engaging.

The two were a magnificent match and devoted to making the other happy. They eventually had twin boys, and somewhere along the way their sparkling affection began to tarnish. Moments of pleasure were replaced with times of plotting. They each chose a son to privately adore and endorse (Gen. 25:28; 27:1–30).

What turned this marriage into a masquerade? How did they go from walking in the same direction to turning in opposite ones? When did they stop growing together and start growing apart? It happened when the communication between the two diminished. Someone left the hallway cluttered.

We know it takes two to tango, but let's just look at what

the Bible reveals. Rebecca inspired her youngest son to plot against her husband in order to steal her eldest son's birthright. Now, she didn't do this out of spite for her eldest, nor out of maliciousness toward her husband; she was trying to follow the prophecy of God (Gen. 25:22–23).

However, the problem is this: she should have communicated what the Lord had told her concerning her sons to her husband instead of sneaking around. As a result of not communicating, their family was divided by deception.

My friend, don't allow their mistake to be your own. Interact with your spouse by keeping in mind the five talks in communication. Doing this will move you beyond merely communicating to connecting.

With its tall towers and famous red paint job, the Golden Gate Bridge quickly became a famous American landmark and a symbol of San Francisco. The History Channel Web site notes,

The enormous towers and vibrant red color have made the Golden Gate Bridge a celebrated American landmark and the pride of San Francisco. The Golden Gate Bridge defied the popular opinion of its day, which said it could not be constructed. Billions of vehicles have passed on the famous bridge, and now millions travel across each year.[3]

In order to become tw0ne—two becoming one—we must keep the hallway of our marriage clear of certain *people*, there are *places* we must close, and we must allow our communication to clean up unnecessary *things*. By doing this, the hallway of our marriage will be like the Golden Gate Bridge, a strong connection and a spectacle to see.

THE MASTER BEDROOM

I love sleep. My life has the tendency to fall apart when
I'm awake, you know?
—ERNEST HEMINGWAY

Chapter Six

The Rest of the Story

MANY WOULD DECLARE "The Rumble in the Jungle" as boxing's crowning jewel. Without question it certainly was a title bout of enormous magnitude. The brawl set the undisputed heavyweight champion, George Foreman, against the former heavyweight champion, Muhammad Ali.

Foreman, who was the younger opponent at age twenty-five, was widely feared for his powerful body-pounding ability. Ali, who was thirty-two years old, was known for his cat-like quickness, but was believed to be in his declining years.

From the sound of the bell, Foreman wasted no time dishing out punishment to Ali. The younger fighter hurled one haymaker after another, while Ali seemed content to just last through the early rounds.

Ali may have seemed whipped from the start, but he had what he considered a secret weapon. His weapon was named by his trainer as the "rope-a-dope," because Ali planned to lean on the ropes while Foreman thundered blow after blow. Ali's trainer joked that only a dope would use a strategy like that.[1]

Ali's strategy was an ultimate game of cat and mouse, and eventually it would begin to show signs of paying off. Soon a noticeably fatigued Foreman began receiving some punishment of his own. Ali tactically covered himself and with precision landed hits to Foreman's face, leaving noticeable wounds.

The plan of the aged Ali materialized as he rested and relied on the ropes and Foreman's flurries began to sap his energy. After several rounds the fight presented a twist of suspense leaving spectators wondering, "Who would win this nail-biting brawl?"

In the ring of life, we must not overlook the importance of the bedroom. The bedroom is often viewed as a place of intimacy, but the aspect often neglected is the place of rest. For that reason, I decided to forgo discussing the topic of sex. Although sex is an important element in the marriage, I feel it is more needful to focus on the rest needed to sustain the marriage. (I have dedicated a chapter to the topic of sex in my book *Marriage Matters: For Better or Worse*.)

Sleep is essential for a person's health and well-being. Yet, millions of people do not get enough of it. Many marriages are on edge because one or both partners suffer from sleep deprivation. Just as the master bedroom is the core of any house, sleep is central for a healthy marriage. Therefore, we want to consider the demand, danger, and duty of rest.

THE DEMAND OF REST

> Six days shall work be done: but the seventh day is the sabbath of rest, an holy convocation; ye shall do no work therein: it is the sabbath of the LORD in all your dwellings.
>
> —LEVITICUS 23:3

Getting rest is of such importance that God placed a demand on it. What's more, God Himself, after six days of work, rested on the seventh day (Gen. 2:2). There is no evidence that God blessed any of the other days, yet He blessed the seventh day (Gen. 2:3). In the account given, every day had a beginning and an ending with the exception of the seventh day. The seventh day (God's rest) began, but it never ended. This is to say, God wants us to remain in His rest.

Spiritually speaking, to remain in God's rest means to trust Him with our lives and in the daily duties we perform. Also, His demand to rest connotes we must take time to rest our bodies to avoid breakdowns and burn-outs.

In the Hebrew culture, they celebrate the sabbath. Our

word *sabbath* comes from a Hebrew word meaning "to cease from your works; to rest." Moses gave the commandment that weekly rest was given to servants and animals (Exod. 23:12). Thus, keeping the sabbath is considered a humanitarian act. The Lord also demanded that His people observe every seventh year as a Sabbatical year which would allow the land to rest (Lev. 25). If God is concerned about rest for the land, you know He wants rest for the man.

In order for the marital union to last long and maintain a strong structure the couple must have rest. There is no two ways about it. The person who is worn out is no good to themselves or their family.

A pastor friend of mine decided to see a medical professional because he suffered from insomnia. His doctor asked him to describe his bedroom. Proudly, my friend boasted of his bookcase that held his favorite studying materials. Then he explained that his wife had a sewing machine positioned in the corner of the room. His eyes lit up as he bragged about his fifty-two-inch flat screen on the wall. Suddenly, his physician stopped him and said, "I've heard enough." My friend countered, "But, I wanted to mention my surround sound." His doctor assured him that she had heard enough. Then she told him his insomnia was stimulated by everything in his bedroom except the bed.

She then advised him to get rid of all that stuff from his bedroom, starting with the fifty-two-inch flat screen. The doctor went on to say that the bedroom is reserved for intimacy and rest.

I tried to implement the no-TV rule in my bedroom, but Andrea was not buying it. Every morning she complained of not getting enough rest, and I conveyed it would help to rid the room of the television. In recent years we've made progress. She now turns the TV off when she's intending on sleeping, whereas in times past she would fall asleep with it on. As a result of that, Andrea has noted her sleep has been a lot better.

The following diagram will give four top reasons why sleep is critical for a person.[2]

Chronic Sleep Deprivation and Its Effects	
Health	Alters immune functions, weight gain, hypertension, and other related diseases
Safety	Daytime sleepiness, possibly causing danger in the working environment and/or traffic accidents
Cognitive	Difficulty remembering and concentrating
Mood	Emotional stress, irritability, impatience

God the Father knows best. He created the human anatomy and therefore knows how it works. Get this: God designed our body to repair itself while we sleep. So, when we deprive ourselves from sleep we're denying our bodies the appropriate maintenance needed to function at a high level. God did not suggest we get rest; He demanded us to receive it.

Even with the demand of rest, we must be aware of the danger of too much rest.

THE DANGER OF REST

How long wilt thou sleep, O sluggard? when wilt thou arise out of thy sleep?...The sluggard will not plow by reason of the cold; therefore shall he beg in harvest, and have nothing.

—PROVERBS 6:9; 20:4

When God gave the command to rest He wasn't giving us permission to become couch potatoes. Quite the contrary. He expects us to work. In fact, He gave the very first job to Adam (Gen. 2:15).

Rest is beneficial, but too much of it is detrimental. God created us to work. Rest rejuvenates us so we may fulfill our assignments with joy.

There are three fundamentals of joy. They are having something to do, someone to love, and something to look forward to in the future. The person who places too much emphasis on rest will disqualify himself from all three. An overdose of rest is called laziness. The lazy person is not looking for anything to do. He loves only himself and should not anticipate a good-looking future.

> One day I walked by the field of an old lazybones, and then passed the vineyard of a lout; They were overgrown with weeds, thick with thistles, all the fences broken down. I took a long look and pondered what I saw; the fields preached me a sermon and I listened: "A nap here, a nap there, a day off here, a day off there, sit back, take it easy—do you know what comes next? Just this: You can look forward to a dirt-poor life, with poverty as your permanent houseguest!"
> —PROVERBS 24:30–34, THE MESSAGE

Wow! The previous text says it all. Too much rest becomes dangerous. Before he knows it, the lazy person is standing face to face with poverty.

Jesus told a parable about a man who planted wheat. While the man was asleep his enemy came and planted weeds. The man's field had been damaged, and it happened while he was sleeping. The devil is known for making sneak attacks. He never confronts you to your face. He is known as the father of lies and the deceiver.

Be on guard! If you're currently unemployed and you're

able to work, look for a job. If you have been searching for a job, keep believing God will open the right door to employment.

Some people only want an unemployment check because they see it as easy money. They say, "This is money without the hassle of working." Listen, there's nothing wrong with receiving unemployment. We all need a helping hand, but there is something wrong with the person who lives with his hand out.

Never be too proud to work. Sometimes you have to start at the bottom positions in order to operate in top places. I've had previous jobs that didn't appear to have anything to do with God's ultimate plan for my life. I've been a shoe salesman, dish washer, soldier in the military, and a forklift operator. I believe every occupation in some way has worked together to prepare me for God's purpose for my life.

The same can be said concerning Joseph in the Bible. He worked many jobs—most against his will—before God brought him to his ultimate position as the deputy to Pharaoh, the ruler of Egypt.

I've discovered one of the greatest joys is not what we do apart from our work but what we get to do with our work. Every one of us touches the life of someone else in some way. Let's not squander our God-given opportunities with laziness.

A poem from *McGuffey's Eclectic Primer* that is applicable for all in life is:

> Work while you work,
> Play while you play;
> One thing each time,
> That is the way.
>
> All that you do,
> Do with your might;
> Things done in halves
> Are not done right.[3]

Rest is certainly in order, but we must not be given to slothfulness. We must be wise in our rest and not neglect our duties.

THE DUTY OF REST

Come to me and I will give you rest—all of you who work so hard beneath a heavy yoke. Wear my yoke—for it fits perfectly—and let me teach you; for I am gentle and humble, and you shall find rest for your souls; for I give you only light burdens.

—MATTHEW 11:28, TLB

While celebrating their thirtieth wedding anniversary a couple sat in a nice restaurant to reflect on the passing years. The wife carefully removed her husband's glasses and noted, "You know, Babe, without your glasses you look like the same handsome young man I married thirty years ago." While smirking, the husband remarked, "Without my glasses, you still look young and pretty also!"

It is encumbered upon the couple to be at rest with one another and not disturb one another's rest. I have found the best way to do this is through reflection and levity.

Too often we bring the burdens of the workplace home with us, and this is in total violation of the order of things. We call it *the workplace* for a reason. It's the place where we work, and therefore it's the place where work should stay.

Now, there are cases when our jobs must be completed at the house, but this should be the exception, not the norm. Some may even work from the house, and if so, there should be a room set aside for your work. Therefore, at some point during the evening you can leave the work in your office at home and close the door.

We have been given a duty to rest for the sake of longevity for our lives and for our marriage. All work and no rest will upset the order of things and eventually wear us out. Too much work can cause stress and worry.

> He will defy the Most High God and wear down the saints with persecution, and he will try to change all laws, morals, and customs.
> —DANIEL 7:25, TLB

The devil will try to change all laws, morals, and customs. When I was growing up it wouldn't be a strange thing to see the majority of stores closed on Sunday. It was a custom for people to take that day off for rest. Nowadays, people can barely attend church because their job schedules them to work on Sunday. This is the devil's way of changing customs.

This same philosophy has crept into our homes, where we feel there's no time for rest. Sooner or later, not resting catches up to you. The bedroom of your marriage demands that you take time out to enjoy each other.

Here's my philosophy: Don't work for a living and never enjoy the life you were given. Then your health is taken, and you can't enjoy the money you were making.

The Bible records a man who concerned himself with making hoards of money, but his result was unfavorable.

> Then he told them this story: "The farm of a certain rich man produced a terrific crop. He talked to himself: 'What can I do? My barn isn't big enough for this harvest.' Then he said, 'Here's what I'll do: I'll tear down my barns and build bigger ones. Then I'll gather in all my grain and goods, and I'll say to myself, Self, you've done well! You've got it made and can now retire. Take it easy and have the time of your life!' Just then God showed up and said, 'Fool! Tonight you die. And your barnful of goods—who gets it?'"
> —LUKE 12:16–20, THE MESSAGE

Beloved, at some point stop running and start resting.

David, who was the king of Israel, had to find the importance of rest. While running to avoid conflict with his son, he is well noted for saying, "The LORD is my Shepherd; I shall not want. He maketh me to lie down" (Ps. 23:1–2). There are times when the Lord will make us lie down because rest is necessary.

Jacob, running from his brother, Esau, had come to a place of rest. And when he did, he saw God in a vision. He witnessed the angels of the Lord ascending and descending from Earth to the heavens (Gen. 28:11–16). We may think we're in it alone, but when we take the time to rest, God reveals His hand is there helping us along the way.

God told Moses, who was running from the Pharaoh's reach, to take off his shoes (Exod. 3:5), and He's commanding us to do the same. Kick off your shoes; lay back with your spouse. Stop looking for the Lord to do; start appreciating what the Lord has done.

As we revisit "the Rumble in the Jungle" let's fast-forward to the eighth round. Foreman was noticeably fatigued, and at that point, like a sleeping giant, Ali awakened and commenced to let Foreman have it. Ali hit Foreman with one heavy chop after another.

The crowd was stunned, and Foreman staggered as his legs gave out from under him and he collapsed on the canvas. Eventually, Foreman stood up, but he could not withstand Ali's onslaught; the referee stopped the bout with two seconds remaining in the round.[4]

Against insurmountable odds, Ali was able to do what many thought he couldn't. He found victory not in his masterful maneuvers; his victory came because he knew when to rest. By using the ropes, he was able to absorb the pounding and punishment given by his opponent and stand as champion in the end.

Ali famously said in an earlier fight, "I shocked the world!"

However, in this fight he *showed* the world. He showed us all the proper technique when facing the challenges this world presents. The strategy for victory is not how well we can work and maneuver only; it's in knowing when to rest on the ropes.

Take care. After this chapter I need some rest, and so do you.

THE BATHROOM

Take care of your body. It's the only place you have to live.

—JIM ROHN

Chapter Seven

Check Yourself

WILLIAM HENRY HARRISON was the ninth president of the United States. His road to the White House was long and hard fought. In fact, he was sixty-eight years old when inaugurated, the oldest president to take office at that time.[1]

In his earlier years he was a decorated officer and he made his greatest victory against the Shawnee tribes that would be famously labeled The Battle of Tippecanoe. Harrison's victory over the tribal forces catapulted him to the national stage and made him a hero in the eyes of many.

Harrison served as a governor and later as a U.S. congressman and senator. His copious congressional experiences set the stage for him to eventually take the office as the U.S. president.

While on the campaign trail, Harrison had gained notoriety for being too old and weak for the presidential office. His critics cracked one joke after another even claiming he was a fake Andrew Jackson.

Although Harrison defeated his opponent for the Oval Office, he still felt he had much to prove concerning his strength and ability to lead the country at his age. Therefore, he made the decision not to wear a coat and hat on an extremely cold and wet day. This folly would prove fatal.

On March 4, 1841, Harrison delivered the longest inaugural address in American history. As a result of inclement weather at his inauguration and his resolve not to dress appropriately, Harrison caught a bad cold that quickly became pneumonia. Harrison died on his thirty-first day in office, serving the shortest tenure in United States presidential history.

Usually from the first date on, we are accustomed to

checking out our spouse. We learn their mannerisms and certain idiosyncrasies that make them unique. We discover their quirks and qualities through close observation. This is fine, but at some point we must shift the focus from our spouse to ourselves.

Any good contractor knows there's no sense in building a house without a bathroom. I, for one, would love a home theater in my house complete with huge recliners, an optimum screen, and concessions. A home theater is fantastic as a request, but it's not a requirement. These days, a bathroom is required.

The bathroom is the place to relieve and reflect. Of the entire house, the bathroom is where you can assuredly be alone. The bathroom is private and personal, a place for introspection and correction. In short, it's the room where you check yourself.

Every marriage must provide the space for couples to check themselves. The areas we must maintain are sanity, sanctity, and sanitation.

Look for Sanity

> When he finally came to his senses, he said to himself, "At home even the hired servants have food enough to spare, and here I am dying of hunger!"
> —Luke 15:17, nlt

Life has a gravitational pull and can depress us if we allow it. For some, times are hard and appear to be getting harder. If all we see are bills piling high and resources plummeting low, we can become disgusted and despondent. Sometimes the issues in the home can weigh more than problems that occur outside the house.

Such was the case with a young man in the Bible. The Scriptures don't indicate it, but there were issues definitely taking place in his house. We know this because he had an uncaring, belligerent elder brother.

This young man demanded money of his father so he could strike out on his own. The father capitulated, and the young man set out. It wasn't long before he squandered his fortune on riotous living.

Feeling down and dejected, now all alone, the son came to his senses (Luke 15:17). While isolated, he realized things were better at home. Sure, his family had its failures, but not beyond repair.

It's good for couples to spend time together, but then there are moments when it's healthy to be alone. There is such a thing as being too close for comfort. Living with anyone twenty-four seven requires taking breaks, or you'll reach your breaking point.

If we are honest, the problem is not always with our spouse or others in the household. Sometimes the problem resides within us. The Bible conveys that when the young man was by himself he came to his senses.

We all have experienced moments of insanity. Now, it may not have been categorized as a clinical illness, but we've been there. Sometimes your children will cause you to make a choice between incarceration and isolation. Maybe you and your spouse have had your share of verbal bouts. If so, next time rather than losing your mind, find peace in the bathroom. In there, the close-to-insane find their senses.

> And after six days Jesus taketh Peter, James, and John his brother, and bringeth them up into an high mountain apart.
> —MATTHEW 17:1

Jesus took a few of His disciples to a mountain apart from the ruckus. He desires to take us to a place of solitude to keep us sane. Jesus takes us up and apart so when we come down we won't fall to pieces.

This world can drive a lot of people insane. Oftentimes there are reports of people losing their cool. Therefore, we can't always wait until we're about to blow a fuse before we take a moment for rest and reflection.

When it comes to people, there is always an implosion before there's an explosion. Meaning, they have experienced a meltdown before deciding to blow up. This can be avoided just by spending time in the metaphoric bathroom.

Sometimes, just head for the restroom, and if you're quiet and patient, you can hear Jesus say, "Peace be still."

LOOK FOR SANCTITY

As often as possible Jesus withdrew to out-of-the-way places for prayer.
—LUKE 5:16, THE MESSAGE

We must check ourselves by getting alone, but before we come out we need to seek the heart and mind of Jesus. Often, Jesus withdrew Himself to connect with God the Father. By doing this, His passion was intense and His purpose straight.

Our times of isolation must be for the purpose of insulation. In other words, we are not to separate from our spouses simply because we're upset. The purpose of getting alone is to receive the Father's heart and mind and to express His love.

But we Christians have no veil over our faces; we can be mirrors that brightly reflect the glory of the Lord. And as the Spirit of the Lord works within us, we become more and more like him.
—2 CORINTHIANS 3:18, TLB

In the bathroom is where you'll find a mirror. We ought not to ignore the image the mirror reflects. This is time for introspection and correction.

Whenever I counsel troubled marriages, without fail I seek to shift the focus where it belongs—on God. Couples come in distraught because they have spent the majority of their time looking at one another. Then they want to spend the counseling session discussing the other's faults.

However, I reveal to them that the purpose of the session is to see their situation from God's perspective. Now, it becomes difficult to see things God's way if they cannot see the Lord. They need the Lord's viewpoint concerning their marriage. The way to receive God's perspective is by reading His Word.

God's Word is a defense in a world that defies His Word. Therefore, if we are not in His Word, more than likely we are headed in the wrong direction.

Whenever we encounter stagnation in the relationship, we must check ourselves. With God, everything is alive and productive. If we wake up one morning and, for no just cause, decide we no longer love our mates, we must check out our devotion to God.

A devotion to God causes a dependence on His Spirit and a dedication to His Word. God the Father loves your spouse. Hence, if His Spirit dwells in you, you can love your spouse as well. We must read His Word every day and allow it to transform our lives.

How we treat the Word of God determines how we treat the God of the Word. If we can take or leave God's Word, we can do God the same way, and eventually that spirit transfers to our spouse.

> For if a person just listens and doesn't obey, he is like a man looking at his face in a mirror; as soon as he walks away, he can't see himself anymore or remember what he looks like. But if anyone keeps looking steadily into God's law for free men, he will not only remember it but he will do what it says, and God will greatly bless him in everything he does.
> —JAMES 1:23–25, TLB

Simply stated, our marriage will reflect our devotion to God.

The other important element for our sanctity is prayer. Prayer produces intimacy. We become intimate with the one we pray to (God) and also the one we pray with and for (our spouse).

God's Word (the Bible) and our prayer life must be inextricably linked. First, we discover what God says about our situation and then we confess what He says, not what we think. Too many people are not meeting their full potential in their marriages because they are thinking about the problems, as opposed to confessing the solutions.

It's important when we pray to put God in remembrance of His Word concerning our marriage and all the affairs that affect us. No one has ever burned out because of prayer; prayer causes us to burn within and allows us to keep our passion for our spouse.

> And another angel came and stood at the altar, having a golden censer; and there was given unto him much incense, that he should offer it with the prayers of all saints upon the golden altar which was before the throne. And the smoke of the incense, which came with the prayers of the saints, ascended up before God out of the angel's hand.
> —Revelation 8:3–4

It's amazing. God sits upon His throne wanting and waiting to hear from us, so designate that time of sanctity.

Look for Sanitation

> And he put forth his hand, and touched him, saying, I will: be thou clean.
> —Luke 5:13

A major asset is our health. Without our health we can't enjoy many of life's pleasures. We certainly will miss golden opportunities with our spouse if our health is jeopardized. It stands to reason that good health should be a top priority.

The bathroom affords us the opportunity to check ourselves out. Now, I'll admit I'm not the paragon of good health, and therefore, I wanted to omit this topic altogether. Nevertheless, if we are going to check ourselves, health is a topic that needs to be discussed.

I recognize the sensitivity of some of the information in this section; however, the following areas need to be covered for the sake of cleanliness and healthiness:

Eating Properly[2]

- "Don't skip breakfast." Studies show eating breakfast is advantageous toward losing weight. Those who skip breakfast tend to compensate for it later by overeating, especially late in the evening, causing weight gain.

- Don't stop eating. Eating small meals throughout the day, such as fruits and vegetables, curtails the appetite and at the same time allows us to eat properly.

Exercise Regularly[3]

- Start with stretching. Take care to stretch when you get out of bed. While stretching, breathing deeply causes oxygen-rich blood to flow to sore muscles.

- "Experts say weight lifting should be done first" while your strength is at its peak. When doing cardiovascular training, it's best to "set your treadmill or step machine on interval... program[s]." This will give you the best results in the shortest amount of time.

- Athletic activities are always a great way to work out. "Swimming is the most asthma-friendly sport of all."

- If you're able to, "enlist the help...of a personal trainer."

Examine Your Body[4]

Women

- Do regular examinations of your breast. "Have a pap smear once a year....Cervical cancer kills 200,000 women a year," but there's a 100 percent survival rating if detected early.

Men

- Familiarize yourself with the signs of heart disease and respond accordingly. Receive annual examinations for prostate cancer. Men typically avoid the prostate examine to forgo being probed. To those men I reason, "It's better to be seen than viewed."

Note: These are just a few health tips. Above all, make regular appointments with your family physician. If you are without a physician, make it a priority to obtain one.

I read an anecdote depicting some of the ailments people contend with, and I want to share it with you.

> Someone called the number to a psychiatric hotline and received the following menu options:
> - If you are obsessive-compulsive, please press 1 repeatedly.
> - If you are codependent, please ask someone to press 2.
> - If you have multiple personalities, please press

3, 4, 5, and 6.

- If you are schizophrenic, listen carefully and a little voice will tell you which number to press.

- If you are paranoid-delusional, we know who you are and what you want. Just stay on the line while we trace this call.[5]

Listen, everyone has health issues, some more severe than others. The point is this: take the time to check your health so that you may increase your chances of enjoying your spouse and the life you have been given.

While in grade school, I recall one time my teacher gave an exam and decided to allow us to grade our own paper.

This concept caught the entire class totally off guard. I, for one, couldn't believe I would be given the opportunity to grade my own test. I remember thinking, "I can change all of my wrong answers."

Just before the teacher began giving the correct answers; she gave this admonishment: "If by checking yourself you change the answer, you'll be cheating yourself." Her warning hit me like a ton of bricks: "Check yourself; don't cheat yourself." Since then, I have carried that axiom my entire life.

William Henry Harrison only held the office of the President of the United States for thirty-one days because on a very wintery day he failed to dress and act appropriately. On his deathbed he was reported to have said to John Tyler, "Sir, I wish you to understand the true principles of the government. I wish them carried out. I ask nothing more."[6]

What could have been accomplished through William Henry Harrison never was because of recklessness. He failed to check himself. His life is one that ended tragically, yet with an impressionable lesson: If we fail to check ourselves, we only cheat ourselves.

THE GUEST BEDROOM

Love cannot remain by itself—it has no meaning. Love has to be put into action and that action is service.

—MOTHER TERESA[1]

Chapter Eight

At Your Service

EUGENE ALLEN WAS born on July 14, 1919, in the town of Scottsville, Virginia. He grew up under Jim Crow laws and tasted the sting of bitter racial discrimination. As a young man Allen acquired the trade of a waiter, and this humble endeavor brought him all the way to the White House. His initial task at the White House was as a pantry worker, but hard work and attention to detail earned him a promotion to the status of butler.[2]

Allen served as a butler to eight U.S. presidents, beginning with Harry S. Truman. Due to the call of serving, Allen had firsthand knowledge of White House matters during some of our country's most turbulent times. He witnessed many intimate moments and close discussions given by our nation's top leaders. Eugene Allen was a servant at heart, as many would attest. He was said to possess a spirit of humility, as he was quick to serve the aristocratic and the common man alike.

Remarkably, as a butler he was extended an invitation to attend President John F. Kennedy's funeral. However, while deeply hurt over the tragic event, he elected to remain at the White House to accommodate the needs of the many guests who came to pay their respects.

During the Reagan Administration, Allen became maître d' of the White House. As a butler this man accomplished much before finally retiring in 1986.

Mr. Allen did wonders tending to the various needs of our United States presidents, and his story should be an encouragement to us all. Many of us will never serve a president of the United States, but we will have numerous opportunities to serve others. Some people are miserly, while others are munificent.

I can discern much about a person just by looking at their house. A beautifully manicured garden could indicate the owner pays attention to details. Their furniture might reveal if they're uptight or easygoing. Wall hangings tend to convey if they're into family, given to travel, or aficionados of art.

Of all the clues in the home that could display people's personalities, the most is the guest bedroom. Having a guest bedroom connotes a heart of hospitality. It means the home-owner has gone out of the way to ensure that visitors are provided for and made comfortable.

Marriages are truly built to last when couples within the union have hearts to help others as well as each other. Our service to others extends from an appreciation toward God for providing our needs. Couples who give together are able to peacefully live together, because theirs is a relationship built on sacrifice, not selfishness.

Develop Your Caring

Don't be selfish; don't live to make a good impression on others. Be humble, thinking of others as better than yourself. Don't just think about your own affairs, but be interested in others, too, and in what they are doing.

—Philippians 2:3–4, TLB

Caring for others takes a sense of compassion. Compassion is the emotional capacity to feel what others are going through. It compels us to stand with others as they are facing trials and ordeals and are in need of a companion to encourage them along the way.

The propensity to care begins in our heart, but then it enters our mind, meaning we become thoughtful toward seeing others do better. We develop a disposition toward caring and, hence, sharing whatever we have to aid our neighbors through their woes.

All of us were given an innate inclination to care for others;

however, through the harshness of life our caring slowly erodes. Just think, when babies are together in a nursery, if one cries, others let out a chorus of cries. When the baby's pain is felt by the others, a sympathetic river is released.

We must all recommit ourselves to caring for others, starting with our spouse. It's a perversion to attempt to save the world while not being sympathetic to those in our homes.

When God called Moses as an instrument of deliverance for Israel, He didn't want Moses to ignore his family's needs. The Bible records that God was going to kill Moses because in his haste to help others he failed to provide for his son (Exod. 4:24–25). Some of us are gung-ho when it comes to helping strangers but slow of foot when it's time to provide for family.

Unfortunately, I have counseled couples on the verge of divorce. Their marriage was scheduled for demolition due to one too many marital disputes. Many of the arguments that ensue between couples are spawned by a lack of caring. They are aloof to each other's feelings, insensitive toward their spouse's needs. At this point, the development of compassion is necessary.

To develop the capacity to care, one needs to remember and reflect on the fact that no man is an island. First, there must be a recall of one's own pain or needs. Every person has needed help at some point. Even if a person was not born with a silver spoon in their mouth, they can thank God for providing a fork in their hand. When we remember that God loves and cares for us we can reflect that love and care to others.

Thus, to develop the capacity toward compassion, we need only remember we are loved and cared for by the Architect of creation (God). We must be ever mindful to plow away the *isms* that seek to destroy our bowels of compassion: racism, sexism, classism, and the like. This cultivates caring and determines how the Lord entrusts His resources to our charge.

Discover You Can

> If you start thinking to yourselves, "I did all this. And all by myself. I'm rich. It's all mine!"—well, think again. Remember that God, your God, gave you the strength to produce all this wealth.
>
> —Deuteronomy 8:17–18, The Message

In life, I've discovered the only thing greater than *receiving* answered prayer is *being* answered prayer. The Lord gives us many things: love, peace, good health, and financial stability, to name a few. Therefore, it is incumbent upon us to become the Lord's conduits. Instead of asking God to extend His hand, we must become extensions of His hand.

The following poem from *McGuffey's Second Reader* relates true inner beauty that only comes from helping others:

> Beautiful faces are they that wear
> The light of a pleasant spirit there;
> Beautiful hands are they that do
> Deeds that are noble, good and true;
> Beautiful feet are they that go
> Swiftly to lighten another's woe.[3]

There's honestly no feeling like helping another in need. With so much chicanery in the world, we become suspicious of everything and everyone. However, not seizing the opportunity to help others robs us of our God-given assignment.

One day I was conversing with my mother-in-law about God talking to the saints. She revealed a time when God spoke to her personally. One morning Mom was complaining to God about her myriad of tasks. She cried, "Lord, I don't have time to go to this place, I don't have time to see this person, and I don't have time to get this done." Suddenly, the Lord interrupted her wailing: "Rose, you don't have time *to do nothing*."

The same thing the Lord said to my mother-in-law, He

says to us. He did not bless us with time on this earth to sit back and do nothing.

Jesus said if a person asked us to go a mile with them, we should go two, and if they would ask to borrow a thing from us, to give it to them (Matt. 5:41–42). In giving we also discover fulfillment. Jesus told us it is more of a blessing to give to others than to receive from others (Acts 20:35).

Now, I've been on both sides. I have given to people, and I have received from people, and I prefer to give. Being able to give means God has empowered us with the resources to do so.

Having the heart to give does not always mean giving money or materials. It could mean giving people our time. I'm always invited to social events, and I'm truly thankful for every invitation. However, for the most part, there was a time when I would not accept the invite. I figured people were inviting me in order to cover their bases.

On one occasion, my friend's wife extended an invitation for me to attend his surprise birthday party. When I accepted, she was genuinely excited. She expressed how her husband truly liked Andrea and me and would count our presence as a blessing.

That's when I realized giving does not stop with things. Sometimes the greatest gift we can give is ourselves. When we decide to have the heart of generosity and serve others, God gives us the ability to accomplish it.

On a particularly hot and long day, Jesus taught the masses. The people had been listening to Jesus' teaching from morning well into the evening. The time had come when the people needed to eat. Jesus' disciples suggested allowing the people to leave because there were too many to feed. The disciples' intentions seemed fine, but their plan had a major flaw. They wanted to send the people away with their problems, while Jesus wanted to develop them as problem-solvers.

Jesus saw the people's need and the disciples' dilemma; therefore, He told His pupils to feed them (Mark 6:37). In other words, giving should begin within our hearts and then extend to what's in our hands. Jesus was teaching that when it comes to giving *we can!*

After allocating the various loaves to the people, the crowd was fulfilled, and the disciples had enough bread left to store away. When we allow God to use us to give to others, He'll always make sure that there's enough left over for us. God wants us to become a pipe through which He can channel His blessings to people. Never forget: when the water goes through the pipe, the pipe always gets wet.

When it comes to serving others, don't conclude you can't; determine you can. One of Andrea's prayers is to accumulate wealth for the purpose of assisting others. I believe her prayer has been an intricate factor in our financial stability.

We both agree meeting the needs of the people God has placed on our hearts is essential. Therefore, we look to be available when God sends people our way.

DISPENSE WHEN THEY COME

> I will cause you to become the father of a great nation;
> I will bless you and make your name famous, and you
> will be a blessing to many others.
>
> —GENESIS 12:2, TLB

Many people are coming and will need your generosity. The key is in sowing seed, not throwing seed. This means not everyone you come in contact with is sent from God to receive.

When a farmer sows seed, he takes his time to prepare the land as he plants strategically. A person who throws seed has no aim and is expecting no particular harvest. Sowing seed is caring; throwing seed is careless. A sower complements God's will for their life. The thrower complains about God's will for their life.

There is a particular couple that is dear to Andrea and me. This couple has been married for over thirty years, and at some point in their union they hit a rough patch. They decided to come to us for counseling. We shared the heart of God concerning their marriage and prayed with them for their family.

One evening God placed that couple on our hearts. Andrea suggested we buy them two tickets for a Caribbean cruise, and I quickly agreed. The couple had never been on a cruise. They took the trip and had the time of their lives. I would love to think that getaway added splendor to a wonderful marriage.

God sent that couple our way, and our only recourse was to obey. After all, Andrea and I have been on the receiving end of trips like that from others. Hence, who are we to deny God's favor and love to those in need? We realize they were sent to us by God.

Do you need fresh life in your marriage? If so, start looking for those God sends your way. Nothing warms the heart like generosity. You and your spouse will see each other in a different light. Your world won't be consumed with merely getting all you can, canning all you got, sitting on the top, and letting the rest rot. That's a spirit of selfishness, and a marriage never thrives from that spirit.

I often challenge couples with the question, What's the most dangerous fish in the world? They respond with the usual suspects: sharks, piranhas, barracudas, etc. That's when I inform them that the most dangerous fish in the world is *selfish*.

You may not ever see a shark up close, chances of encountering piranhas are slim (and for me no chance), and barracudas may never cross your path. But, all of us have had to deal with *selfish*. This fish can kill your marriage and destroy your life.

Jonah found himself in the belly of the fish for three days and three nights (Jon. 1:17). I know, I know. Some find this account a little difficult to believe. I hear some saying, "How can a man spend three days in a fish?" Honestly, many of us have been in a fish and for a lot longer than three days. Many are in a fish right now. Your marriage may be in a fish while you're reading this book—the *selfish*.

God doesn't want you in this fish. He desires to see your marriage succeed. The way out is through having a heart of generosity. If things are getting a little fishy in your marriage; you can't *get* out; you must *give* out!

The Scriptures say godliness with contentment is great gain (1 Tim. 6:6). There are four phases of progression in life:

- *Not enough:* You're looking for God's support.

- *Just enough:* You have God's supply.

- *More than enough:* You operate from God's surplus.

- *Enough is enough:* Through God, you give with satisfaction.

The Bible speaks of a woman who decided she would prepare a guest bedroom for the man of God:

> "I'm certain," said the woman to her husband, "that this man who stops by with us all the time is a holy man of God. Why don't we add on a small room upstairs and furnish it with a bed and desk, chair and lamp, so that when he comes by he can stay with us?"
> —2 Kings 4:10, The Message

As a result of their hospitality the Lord blessed them tremendously. This couple was without a child and desperately desired to have one. I'm sure they had attempted to have one for quite some time but to no avail. However, because they thought on the need of someone else, God met their desire (2 Kings 4:13–17).

One day their son died prematurely. The woman was

distraught and took her dead son to the man of God. Elisha prayed to God, and the child revived (2 Kings 4:32–37).

When we allow the Lord to use us to bless those He sends our way, there's a blessing in it for us as well. It could be that God is trying to get you out of that "fish." No matter the reason, the blessing God gives won't die, and the devil can't steal it. If he tries, the Lord has a way of bringing it back to life and restoring it anew.

Eugene Allen was a blessed man. He was born on a southern plantation. His journey began in poverty and persecution, but it ended with prosperity and promotion.

Allen served eight U.S. presidents, and while functioning in the office of a butler he was graced by meeting civil rights leader Dr. Martin Luther King Jr. He was also privileged on occasions to travel with the Heads of State, once with President Richard Nixon, and another time with President Jimmy Carter.[4]

Growing up in the horrors of the segregated south, Allen never would have dreamed of one day being in the presence of world leaders and, even more, witnessing an African American receiving the appointment to the highest office in the land. However, that is exactly what happened when Allen received and accepted a VIP invitation to President Barak Obama's inauguration on January 20, 2009. His many years of serving as a butler have brought him great rewards. If faithfully serving presidents can grant Allen honors; think of what serving God can bring us.

Offer that guest bedroom in the house of your marriage. Develop caring, discover you can, and dispense what you have when God sends people your way.

Freely you receive, so freely give (Matt. 10:8).

THE FAMILY ROOM

Once you agree upon the price you and your family must
pay for success, it enables you to ignore the minor hurts,
the opponent's pressure, and the temporary failures.
—VINCE LOMBARDI

Chapter Nine

Birds of a Feather

MANY SPECIES OF birds travel together in flocks. Flocks are formed for various reasons. The main purpose is for protection and provision. Whatever action a bird takes is to ensure its existence.

Birds that move in flocks fare better against potential predators. When a predator looks to strike any bird that's a part of a flock, together the birds can cause a distraction.

Provisions occur in flocks when parent birds protect the young as others in the species search and recover food. This allows the defenseless ones in the flock the opportunity to feed and grow without an immediate threat.

Finally, while in flight, some birds have a tendency to lose their strength. When this occurs, they are able to use the momentum the flock creates with the air to remain in position and keep pace.[1]

As we continue to explore the various rooms of a house, the place I believe to be quite essential is the family room, the place where family comes together.

Marriages are often stretched, strained, or strengthened through family crises. The rigors involved in family can be daunting to many, but the rewards far outweigh the sacrifice.

Marriages tend to fair better when the members of the family flock together. Thus, the marital union should consist of mature individuals who are prepared to provide intimacy, affection, and companionship toward its family members. Moreover, a strong marriage provides stability in doubt, support in darkness, and strength in dysfunction.

> A house is built of logs and stone,
> Of tiles and post and piers;
> A home is built of loving deeds

That stand a thousand years.

—Victor Hugo[2]

Stability in Doubt

This is the case of a man who is all alone, without a child or a brother, yet who works hard to gain as much wealth as he can. But then he asks himself, "Who am I working for? Why am I giving up so much pleasure now?" It is all so meaningless and depressing.

—Ecclesiastes 4:8, nlt

The operative word in life is *forward*. Whatever we do in life, the point of it all is to progress. For many, family becomes the motivating factor, the fuel in the tank, the reason for the toil.

The last thing we need is doubt. Doubt neutralizes progress. It causes us to renege and in some cases revert in life. However, when a husband/father knows he is appreciated, he works harder to provide. When a wife/mother is given love, she will labor more knowing the rewards are worth her effort. As the children are nurtured they are equipped to face many of life's challenges.

The family unit is the backbone of every society. In the beginning God had family in mind. He instructed man to be fruitful and multiply (Gen. 1:28). This was His plan for family. Through family the Earth would be replenished and subdued. When something is subdued it is placed at rest. The world as we know it is in chaos, but the family is designed to set calmness in the storm. Thus, the erosion of the family results in instability in society.

Egypt was a cruel country for the Jews. They were handled without regard and treated without respect. Israel was made to labor under unfair and unrelenting conditions. They had no laws to protect them and no means by which to defend themselves.

They spent four hundred years under the oppression of Egypt's pharaoh and the heels of his soldiers. Beneath all the mistreatment was one silver lining—family. Israel entered Egypt with just over seventy people, but when they departed they numbered over 2 million. In essence, in a violent environment, facing an uncertain future, the family brought stability.

Israel faced many challenges on their diaspora to the Promised Land. They tackled tough terrain. I imagine they endured smoldering days and bone-chilling nights. They suffered through famine and fatigue. And they battled opposing nations at every turn.

At many points they became discouraged about God's plan and were in doubt concerning His intentions. However, the cog that kept the people pushing forward was the clan. The Promised Land was not just a relief for the fatigued; it was a future for their family.

In the dark of night, merchant ships transported tanks across the Atlantic Ocean. Suddenly a storm rolled through, causing the tanks on one of the ships to break free of the restricting chains.

As the vessel struggled through the hostile weather and raging waves, the tanks banged within ship. The catastrophe was causing major damage to the ship's interior. The Ship's captain gave command to the crew to go below and secure the tanks. Of course, there was a struggle, but the ship's mates finally gained the advantage and secured their enormous cargo.

Interestingly, the merchant's ship received more damage from its own cargo inside than it did from the storm's disturbance on the outside.

Usually, we can handle the stresses from without when we are settled and secured within.

> Do not waver, for a person with divided loyalty is as unsettled as a wave of the sea that is blown and tossed by the wind. Such people should not expect to receive anything from the Lord. Their loyalty is divided

between God and the world, and they are unstable in everything they do.

—James 1:6–8, nlt

Every family has it challenges. There are times when doubt causes us to question if this is really worth it. When trouble threatens to tear your family apart, remember, your family is weighing in the balance, so get a grip, stabilize your emotions, and steer forward.

When a house is insulated properly, it's protected from inclement weather. Family should provide the insulation and stability needed to ward off the winds of doubt.

Support in Darkness

Each one of us needs to look after the good of the people around us, asking ourselves, "How can I help?"
—Romans 15:2, The Message

If you could go through life without pain, pressures, or problems, I'm sure you would. Unfortunately, that's not an option afforded anyone. We would all love to live trouble free. I for one can recall many days desiring freedom from stress, struggle, and strain. However, instead of freedom I was given favor. The favor of family has encouraged me through many dark moments.

Whenever I would get down in the dumps or deep in depression, I'd think of my family. God gives us family as a support. They are to lift us when we're low and provide the light in the night.

Support groups are big in our society. You can find them just about anywhere. There are support groups for drug and alcohol addictions, physical and mental health disorders, eating disorders, domestic violence, and much more. Of all the support groups, the one often ignored is the family.

Without a doubt, support needs to begin at home. There's a saying, "Home is where the heart is," and I tend to agree.

I make sure my family knows of my love for them. I never want them to feel someone else cares for their well-being more than me. I believe in asking my wife and children about their day. I express genuine concern when they reveal problems and celebrate with each triumph.

Supporting those in our family takes time. Sometimes people exert so much energy for others that by the time they get home they are exhausted. However, this should not happen; exhausted or not, we must make time for family.

Too much time is spent *making a living* that many are missing out on life. Making a living involves making money, but why make the money if you can't enjoy the family you're making the money for? Your life is a compilation of your family. You are one of many links in your family chain. Let it be said your link was a strong, supportive one.

There will invariably be dark moments in your family's life. Spiritually speaking, sin and darkness are synonymous. The darkness of pornography, adultery, lying, stealing, killing, oppression, drunkenness, and the like is ever present.

When members of the family face darkness, the other members must be there as support. Nevertheless, family members are not a mat to be walked on but a post to lean on.

Hosea and Gomer are biblical examples who exude love and the power of support. Usually, their marriage is given as a testimony of forgiveness, and rightfully so. However, our forgiveness must be coupled with support.

Although their marriage began with much promise, Hosea was a preacher who married an unfaithful woman. God gave His blessing on the union by giving them a son. However, after their first child Gomer began showing signs of dissatisfaction.

Her dissatisfaction developed to disrespect. Gomer spent many nights outside the home in the company of other men. As a result of this dark behavior, she had two more children, neither of whom were her husband's. As far as we know, Hosea hadn't done anything to warrant this abuse.

Nevertheless, by the grace of God he forgave and accepted her back into their home.

Amazingly, Hosea's love was not enough to keep Gomer from revisiting her dark past. She decided to leave him for good. Gomer ran away with her latest lover and eventually was left destitute. Soon, Gomer's dark life caused her to become enslaved.

Many family members have chosen a dark path. When this happens, do we discard them? What about that wayward child? Should we disown them because they chose to walk in the darkness of disobedience and not in the guiding light of their parents' love? We find our answer in this account of Hosea and Gomer.

> Then the LORD said to me, "Go and love your wife again, even though she commits adultery with another lover. This will illustrate that the Lord still loves Israel, even though the people have turned to other gods and love to worship them."
>
> —HOSEA 3:1, NLT

The Lord told Hosea to be there for his wife, just as He is there for Israel. To support our loved ones in the dark times doesn't mean we approve of their behavior; it means we convey no condemnation and show the love of God. A person may ask, "When is enough, enough?" Well, it's when the Lord says it's enough, not when we say it. Hosea was able to go back and support Gomer because God told him to do so. The will of God will never lead us where His grace cannot keep us.

We may not see what the future holds, but we must trust in the God who holds our family's future. As we support one another in the dark times, God will be our guiding light.

STRENGTH IN DYSFUNCTION

> A person standing alone can be attacked and defeated, but two can stand back-to-back and conquer. Three

are even better, for a triple-braided cord is not easily broken.

—ECCLESIASTES 4:12, NLT

We must truly comprehend this: none of us can do what all of us can do; we're better together because we're stronger together.

Birds flock together in order to gather strength from one another. As the wind changes, a tired bird is able to catch the current from the other birds which generates enough energy for it to stay in flight.

This procedure happens to work for families as well. Whenever a member of the family lacks energy or loses focus, the other members should come together to encourage the one in need. At some point we all need to gather strength from someone else. Our strength can come from a spouse, a parent, or a child. We may find strength in words they say or in deeds they do.

Someone may say, "I come from a broken home." Friend, every home is broken in one way or the other. However, dysfunction is not a disqualifier. The answer is not living in a home that's free from problems; it's in having the proper perspective of the problem. I love to say, "Birds never complain about traffic; they merely fly above it."

I say again, dysfunctional families are not disqualified from being used to provide strength to their members. More importantly, they are not disqualified from being used by God or receiving His help. Remember, even biblical families experienced dysfunction.

Adam's family began with blame and eventually produced murder. Adam and Eve ate from the forbidden tree. When confronted by God about their disobedience, Adam blamed Eve, and she shifted attention to a snake in the grass.

This kind of blaming and bickering can continue in a marriage for years. It may have affected how their sons Cain and Abel interacted with each other. Then one day the dysfunction appeared in the form of jealously as Cain murdered Abel (Gen. 4:3–8).

Dysfunction found its way into Abraham's family. It started when Abraham asked his wife to lie about their relationship. Instead of Sarah faithfully performing duties as Abraham's wife, she was forced to pretend to be his sister (Gen. 12:11–13).

Subsequently, Sarah asked Abraham to father a child with another woman and later lived to regret it. This episode left a lot of emotional scars (Gen. 16:1–2; 21:10).

Abraham's grandson, Jacob, didn't fair too well in the home either. Jacob had thirteen kids by four different women, all under the same roof (Gen. 29:31–35; 30:1–24). Now, this guy has to win the first place ribbon for domestic dysfunction.

To make matters worse, Jacob showed preferential treatment to his youngest son, making the brothers madder than a pit-bull eating pepper. To get even, the older brothers sold their younger brother into slavery and told their father he died (Gen. 37:12–35).

In the name of common sense, it would be a good idea not to do any of the things that these families did. However, if your family resembles the dysfunction of the aforementioned, don't count your flaws as failures. Nobody has a perfect family, but we serve a perfect God, and He used these families to do great things. In your family, strengthen one another in the dysfunction and allow God to use your loss for His gain.

One fall, a particular bird decided not to fly south with the flock for the winter. He reasoned that to fly this year would be a waste of time. So, at the appointed time when the flock headed south, he stayed north.

One bitterly cold day he realized his horrible mistake of staying behind. Therefore, he set out, hoping to find his flock. While in the air, the cold winds began to frost his wings. Soon he found himself unable to fly, so he plummeted to the ground and fell into a barn.

The bird cried and complained about his frosted wings. He cried so loudly that a cow heard him. The cow approached the bird to investigate the problem. He saw the bird was frozen, so he stood above the bird and dropped a pile of hot mess on him.

The bird couldn't believe the mess he was in and fussed even louder. Suddenly, the bird realized the mess was warming his wings. However, a bobcat overheard the bird crying about the mess and came over to lick it off him. As the bobcat was licking the bird he swallowed him whole.

There are a few morals to this tale. Not everyone who gets you in a mess is your enemy. Not everyone who gets you out of a mess is your friend. The next time you're in a mess, stop complaining and realize God is in control.

Above all, God gave you a family so you can flock together, stabilize one another in doubt, support each other in the dark, and provide strength to your family in dysfunction.

Remember, in good or bad weather, birds of a feather flock together!

THE STUDY

Every day is a gift from God. Learn to focus on the Giver
and enjoy the gift!
—JOYCE MEYER

Chapter Ten

Focus, Please!

IT WAS AN ordinary morning on September 1928; bacteriologist Alexander Fleming conducted his usual business at St. Mary's Hospital. However, this particular day Fleming had noticed his Petri dishes had been contaminated.[1]

Through further observation, Dr. Fleming noticed a peculiar mold had grown on certain petri dishes. Through the use of his microscope, Fleming was stunned to witness the mold prohibiting the normal growth of certain bacteria.[2]

After weeks of trial and error, Fleming was able to see results with the mold that he never would have imagined. The mold displayed the ability to ward off harmful bacteria. Even more, it possessed the capability to fight against infectious diseases. Above all, Fleming was pleased to find the mold was non-toxic.

As it turned out, Fleming's mystery mold was the "wonder drug" penicillin, but the doctor was unaware of this outstanding fact. Fleming's experiments with the drug were simply documented and filed away and went unnoticed for virtually a decade. However, it would later resurface and change the course of medicine forever.

We have now come to the room in our marriage called the study. This is the place where we must stop and consider the course of our marriage and reflect on the events that have taken place. However, keep in mind it is not for us to painstakingly ponder the negative occurrences but rather gratefully contemplate the positives.

The negative events are there to test our marital union's integrity. Anyone can love when all things are bright and blissful, but the true test begins when times are dark and dismal. Love isn't cheap; it costs us everything we have to gain it and give it.

You may be one deliberating divorce. You may think your marriage is infected with mold. If so, don't discount the mold. Examine it! You may discover it is the antidote to counteract the negatives and reactivate your love. Examination of our marriage takes the use of a telescope, microscope, and kaleidoscope.

USE THE TELESCOPE

> Hope deferred maketh the heart sick: but when the desire cometh, it is a tree of life.
>
> —PROVERBS 13:12

The telescope is an interesting instrument because it causes objects that are dark and distant to seem brighter and nearer. It has the capability of placing the out-of-sight in our field of view.

Like the telescope, hope causes the dark and distant to become bright and near. Right now, marriages are suffering because couples have somehow lost hope. They no longer believe in each other. Consequently, they see no hope of a positive outcome in their marriage. The mold has taken its toll, and the partners are left sorting through particles of doubts, disappointments, and neglected duties.

However, there is hope—through the telescope. The couple just needs to refocus. They must not look to one another; they must make the commitment to focus on God. God not only gives us hope; He is our hope.

God has promised to never leave or forsake us (Heb. 13:5). He has promised to give us abundant life (John 10:10). Sure, you may not have all the answers to your problems now, but God's children live off His promises not His explanations.

Abraham was given a promise by God in the form of a vision (Gen. 15:1–4). The promise was that God would reward him with an heir. This heir would be the first of many counted toward Abraham's faith and their friendship.

The Scripture records after God made this promise to His friend, He instructed Abraham to prepare animals for their covenant. In early Jewish culture, it was customary when a covenant was made that each individual would walk through divided beasts.

After Abraham prepared the animals on the altar, birds came to feast on the remains. Abraham spent all day fighting to keep the fowl away. The Bible reveals it wasn't until dark that God, like a smoking furnace, came between the divided pieces (Gen. 15:17).

After Abraham was tired of trying to make the covenant work, in the darkest hour, God showed up. When God gives us a promise, He doesn't expect us to work it out; He's just waiting to see if we will keep our eyes on Him through the telescope of hope.

I remember a story I heard about an experiment on the power of hope. Researchers studied the response of mice in certain situations. They placed one lab mouse in a tub of water and put the tub in a dark room.

They timed it to see how long the mouse would swim in total darkness. The mouse made it just over a couple of minutes before giving up. Then the researchers placed a second mouse in the same tub of water; however, this time they allowed the room's light to remain on. The mouse in the light swam significantly longer than the mouse in the dark.

The reason for the dramatic difference is hope. The mouse with no light had no hope. Looking into total darkness disparagingly gave the first mouse no reason to continue swimming. Like the mouse in the dark, when you stop seeing the positive and stop believing, you give up on your marriage.

When it appears your marital goals are covered with mold, and there's no light in the night, use the telescope of hope.

USE THE MICROSCOPE

These hard times are small potatoes compared to the coming good times, the lavish celebration prepared for us. There's far more here than meets the eye. The things we see now are here today, gone tomorrow. But the things we can't see now will last forever.

—2 CORINTHIANS 4:17–18, THE MESSAGE

The microscope's unique quality allows us to see microscopic matter in a magnified manner. Objects that go undetected to the naked eye are brought into view and given clarity.

Life is filled with trouble, but one thing is true and often overlooked: there are more blessings than problems. Many have a propensity to focus on the negatives, and this simply is not wise for building a strong marriage. Any problem, if viewed closely enough or long enough, will seem larger than what it really is.

Let's do an exercise. If you have a quarter, place it in your hand. Close one eye, and hold the coin close to the open eye. As you stare only at that coin, it will eventually eclipse all other objects. Now, in reality the coin is not larger than the other objects, so how was it able to cover them? The coin concealed the other objects because of your focus. As you concentrated only on the coin its mass was magnified.

Many people magnify their problems. They focus on arguments and negative exchange. On the other hand, when they consider that there are more blessings than problems, they'll use the microscope of praise to detect those things that are not easily seen.

To praise something or someone is to magnify the event or individual. The plan of the devil is to steal your praise. Instead of praising, he wants you pouting. There's no need to soak and sour about your situation.

The Bible speaks of a woman by the name of Hagar. She was an Egyptian slave who joined the caravan of Abraham.

Hagar had no idea who God was or where her life was headed. Leaving Egypt meant one thing for sure: a fresh start.

One day she was instructed to have a child with her master. No one cared for her feelings toward the matter, only for her ability to carry what another couldn't. Out of obedience she gave birth to Abraham's first child, a son by the name of Ishmael.

As the child grew, her contribution to the family was overshadowed by God's promise. Rather than accepting the will of God, she chose to despise it. As a result, she and her child were placed in a predicament that appeared to possibly have a negative conclusion.

Now, Hagar was without family and had no means to provide water for her thirsty son. As her child cried out, Hagar was crying from within.

> Meanwhile, God heard the boy crying. The angel of God called from Heaven to Hagar, "What's wrong, Hagar? Don't be afraid. God has heard the boy and knows the fix he's in. Up now; go get the boy. Hold him tight. I'm going to make of him a great nation." Just then God opened her eyes. She looked. She saw a well of water. She went to it and filled her canteen and gave the boy a long, cool drink.
> —GENESIS 21:17–19, THE MESSAGE

This account always fascinates me. First of all, Hagar felt discarded and disappointed about her present state. Just when she felt as low as one could get, she received a call and not just any call. She would have been elated to receive a call from home, but more than that, she got a call from heaven.

Beloved, when you think you're alone and no one cares, know that God cares. He sees your effort and has a relief plan for your predicament.

This calls to mind the second reason Hagar's account excites me. Hagar was so focused on her present problem she neglected to notice her blessing. As she and the child desperately needed water, the Bible says God opened her eyes. Did you catch that? The Scripture did not convey that God provided a well. No, the well was already there. Hagar couldn't see the bigness of the well because she focused only on the problem. To her, the well paled in comparison to the problem; to God, the problem paled in comparison to the well. Do you see your situation through Hagar's eyes or the eyes of God?

The microscope of praise causes us to look beyond the mold and see God. God causes us to see that all is *well*.

USE THE KALEIDOSCOPE

> Beautiful jewels were inlaid into the walls to add to the beauty.
>
> —2 CHRONICLES 3:6, TLB

The kaleidoscope's fascinating ability allows us to view images in a beautifully multicolored way. Unlike other scopes, the kaleidoscope has many different sides, each allowing another perspective and featuring an additional splendor. To simply see the world in terms of black and white is not to see the world at all.

If your marriage appears mundane, it's only because you're not viewing it through the kaleidoscope of excitement. The kaleidoscope transforms the mundane into the magnificent, the dull to sheer delight, and brings the dead back to life. It allows us to see ordinary objects in an extraordinary way.

Leslie B. Flynn writes this anecdote:

> A wealthy woman who was traveling overseas saw a bracelet she thought was irresistible, so she sent her husband this cable: "Have found wonderful bracelet. Price $75,000. May I buy it?" Her husband promptly wired back this response: "No, price too high." But

the cable operator omitted the comma, so the woman received this message: "No price too high." Elated, she purchased the bracelet. Needless to say, at her return her husband was dismayed. It was just a little thing—a comma—but what a difference it made![3]

Like the comma, the kaleidoscope allows us to pause in life long enough to notice the beauty. When we rush to work, rush to raise the children, and rush in and out of each day, we rush through a life of beauty only to see a blur. This kind of fast pace turns a good marriage into a mirage. One day we find ourselves in union without unity.

God took Ezekiel to a valley filled with dry bones and asked him, "Can these dry bones live?" (Ezek. 37:3, author's paraphrase). Now, in a black-and-white world, with a pale perspective, the obvious answer is no. However, Ezekiel knew enough about God to know that He sees things only in living color. Therefore, Ezekiel's reply was, "Oh Lord God, thou knowest."

God told Ezekiel to speak over the dry bones and to proclaim life and not death over their condition. In essence, God allowed Ezekiel to see through rose-colored glasses. When the prophet looked again, he saw bones being covered with flesh and the bodies coming together as new.

See your marriage not in black and white but in living color. Use the kaleidoscope of excitement to declare life, not death, over your relationship. If your marriage is in calamity or headed for collapse, you can reverse the curse by seeing with the color of God's love.

In the dark, objects appear colorless. However, the items have color that is difficult to detect. A light is needed in order to see color. Don't allow the dark shroud of disappointment and disillusion to convince you the color of hope and help is gone. Get excited knowing weeping endures for a night, but joy (brilliance and beauty) comes in the morning (Ps. 30:5).

Not too long ago I owned a thirty-five millimeter camera. Whenever I took pictures I had to send my roll of film out to be developed. It took the developer some time to produce the photos. Each picture was developed in a dark room. When the process was complete my pictures were returned to me with a major addition—negatives.

Now, all I wanted were the photos. However, every picture had its own negative. I framed many pictures, but never the negatives. I never asked for the negatives but was given them anyhow.

God has a photo of your marriage. You may see the negative of your current condition. Don't focus on the negative. See the beauty of the picture God has for your marriage.

In 1940, over a decade after Alex Fleming's experiments with penicillin halted, two scientists at Oxford University (Howard Florey and Ernst Chain) began new works with penicillin. They were able to create a way to sustain the drug for longer periods of time.[4]

As a result, penicillin was immediately rushed to the soldiers fighting in World War II. It saved many lives and proved to be effective in combating bacterial infections and other incurred wounds. Penicillin was also instrumental in treating diseases such as gangrene, pneumonia, syphilis and tuberculosis.

The discovery of penicillin marked a true turning point in medical history. And to think the discovery came unintentionally by noticing mold through a microscope.

Whenever you stop to study your marriage, ponder only the positives. My friend, don't focus on the negatives. Use the telescope of hope, the microscope of praise, and the kaleidoscope of excitement.

It took scientist over a decade to discover the value in penicillin. If you've found mold in your marriage, give it time, and you'll discover its hidden value as well.

THE OFFICE

If you want to reap financial blessings, you have to sow financially.
—JOEL OSTEEN

Chapter Eleven

Making Money Count

ONCE THERE LIVED an ant and a grasshopper in a grassy meadow. Without fail the ant labored long difficult days. His toil consisted only of traveling back and forth carrying bundles of wheat in order that he could eat during winter. The days were arduous and hot, but that never deterred the ant from the task at hand. Although it was summer, he knew winter was coming, and then it would be too late to seek his food.[1]

On the other hand, the grasshopper spent his summer days in leisure. Whenever the grasshopper took time to notice the ant he would inquire, "Why waste your summer with hard work?" Then the grasshopper advised, "Spend your days like me in leisure, laughter, and laziness."

The ant ignored the pretentious grasshopper and worked faster, harder, and longer. This caused the grasshopper to shuck and jive even more. He didn't consider for one second that winter was coming, for he only lived in the moment.

Soon, nature changed faces from summer to winter. The blazing hot days transformed to dark, bitter, and cold. The sun's rays were replaced with frost and snow.

The pompous grasshopper was now too cold to play. Hunger pangs were his nagging reminder of the wasted summer season. With no food or heat the foolish grasshopper wailed and worried, "Oh what shall I eat? Where shall I go?" Suddenly, he remembered the ant.

As we walk the halls of our marriage and consider the rooms of the house, I think it necessary to visit the office. This is the room to conduct the marital business. In particular, we need to discuss the family's finances.

Managing a house is serious business. As mature adults we must take into account the various details and duties that are involved in ensuring the needs of the family. Money is the tool used to meet these needs. There is one principle to consider when handling money: play or pay. The *play or pay* principle is simple; if you play now, you pay later. On the other hand, if you pay now, you play later.

The goal of this chapter is not to make you rich. However, the principles of this chapter, if applied, can make you rich. My primary focus is to give guidance in the area of finances and to demonstrate the mastery of money for the security of your marriage.

Research has indicated one of the top three reasons for divorce is money. The question then becomes, Is money a marriage menace? If so, it doesn't have to be. The true threat is an improper mind-set concerning money, making money, and managing money.

MIND YOUR MONEY: HOW TO SEE IT

For the love of money is the root of all evil: which while some coveted after, they have erred from the faith, and pierced themselves through with many sorrows.

—1 TIMOTHY 6:10

The scripture reads, "For the *love* of money is the root of all evil" (emphasis added). I've heard someone remark, "For the *lack* of money is the root of all evil." Personally, I can see from both perspectives. Whether we're discussing the *love* or the *lack* of money, we need to master it and not allow money to control us.

In order to master money, we must have the proper mind-set about it. Money must be viewed in two ways: a means and a measure.

Money is anything that is regularly used in exchange. In other words, money is not the end; it is merely the means to the end. Let's say your desire is to own a particular object. Money is not the object; it's only the means by which you obtain the object.

So, in the world's system money is a means, but in the

kingdom of God money is a measure. We can talk about our love for God, but at the end of the day, the litmus test of our love is measured by our money. If we see money properly, we see it as a measure first, not just as a means.

As a measure, money is called and considered the tithe. The tithe is 10 percent of a person's income. The Lord has instructed His people to give Him the tithe. The purpose of the tithe was to indicate God owns it all (Lev. 27:30). Many of God's people view their money as 10 percent belonging to God and 90 percent belonging to them. This is a flawed point of view. The proper perspective is 100 percent belongs to God, and we give Him 10 percent to indicate that fact, while we use the other 90 percent as good stewards.

Couples who tithe together enjoy the blessings of God in their union. Even more, they walk in God's divine favor knowing their giving pleases the Lord. As we trust the Lord with our giving, He causes our money to increase in ways we would not imagine. He sustains our possessions by keeping them from breaking down or becoming depleted altogether (Mal. 3:10–11).

In addition, God tells us to tithe in order to keep us from idolatry. Idolatry causes us to love the gifts more than the Giver. It also robs God from His glory and His people from receiving their God-given rewards (Luke 6:38).

Opponents of tithing argue that this is an act of the Law associated only with the Old Testament. However, tithing was actually instituted prior to the Law and was later written within the Law.

Abraham was approached by two kings. One was Bera, king of Sodom, the other, Melchizedek, king of Salem. Sodom represented the world's prosperity, and Salem stood for God's peace. King Melchizedek brought God's blessings, and Abraham honored the Lord by giving the tithe (Gen. 14:20). King Bera offered the spoils, but Abraham rejected the goods (Gen. 14:23).

Tithing is an act of our worship through obedience, not

mere observance of the Law. This is our way of saying we prefer God's blessings over the world's possessions. In the Old Testament the Israelites had to obey in order to receive God's blessings. However, in the New Testament the people of God obey because they have God's blessings. If the Old Testament believers gave according to the Law; we of the New Testament ought to give according to God's grace (2 Cor. 9:6–15).

When we see that money belongs to God and allow Him to direct our dealings, He will meet every need and provide increase for our desires.

Make Your Money: How to Take It

> Laughter and bread go together, And wine gives sparkle to life—But it's money that makes the world go around.
> —Ecclesiastes 10:19, The Message

My father taught me, "Faith can get you things money can buy; faith can get you things money can't buy; faith can even get you money." Along with faith God gives us His wisdom so that we will know how to accumulate wealth.

As Christians we should not be given to get-rich-quick schemes but to sound financial investments. Jesus taught we should not lay up for ourselves treasures upon the Earth (Matt. 6:19). At first it appears Jesus was teaching not to save or invest our money. On the contrary, He was conveying we should not see money or the things of this world as treasure; rather, we should regard the things of God as treasure. In essence, Jesus wants us to be able to hold money, not hoard it.

Paul taught that through our giving, God will make sure we always have enough for others and every good work (2 Cor. 9:7–12).

Jesus taught about an unjust steward who was in danger of losing his job. He was not a faithful employee (Luke 16:1–7). Being a good steward begins with the willingness to work for wages. If we labor for another, we must be faithful employees. If we are unfaithful with another man's money, God will not give us our own (Luke 16:12).

After we faithfully work and earn money, we must invest it wisely. Through investing we are able to accumulate the wealth we need to provide for our family's future.

There is a biblical parable about a man who gave three servants his money. Two of them invested it, but the third buried the money (Matt. 25:14–18). The two servants who invested their master's money received great rewards (vv. 20–23), but the servant who never invested eventually lost the money he had been given (vv. 24–28).

In life, we better learn the principle of *play or pay.* Remember, if we choose to play now, we will pay later, but if we decide to pay now we can play later. Paying now entails storing up for later. It means creating a savings so there are adequate resources for future needs. This means you may be unable to take vacations right now.

However, your season will come. Playtime will be possible because you diligently invest for financial security. Every household is different, so I won't tell anyone how to invest, but it's important to do so.

The following are some financial vehicles to cover the basics. As your finances change you may need to modify your financial portfolio.

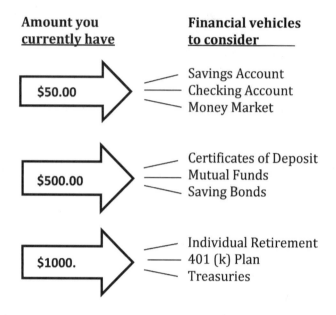

Amount you currently have	Financial vehicles to consider
$50.00	Savings Account / Checking Account / Money Market
$500.00	Certificates of Deposit / Mutual Funds / Saving Bonds
$1000.	Individual Retirement / 401 (k) Plan / Treasuries

The important thing is for you and your spouse to begin saving a portion of the money God places in your hands. Remember, my goal is not to teach on getting rich but to point you in the right direction.

Money does not have to be a sore subject in your marriage. It should be a pleasant topic. Earning and saving should be an exciting endeavor for both partners.

Everyone can save money. You don't need to make a lot in order to save. You can start by saving your change. A habit that I have adopted over the years is to save any change I have left over at the end of the day. The first year I started this, Andrea would chuckle at my efforts to save a little at a time. She would say, "Tyrone, it takes too long to make a signifi-cant amount at the rate you're going." Then one day, at the end of the year, I counted my coins, and it totaled just over eight hundred dollars. When I told Andrea the amount, the next evening she gave me thirty-five cents and said, "Add this with the change *we* already have." When it comes to saving, you can never start too small; the important thing is to just start.

Another great source of financial security is investing in real estate. There's a reason why they call it *real* estate; land will always be valuable. There is just one planet with so much land to go around. If you can get a piece of real estate, it will be to your advantage. The more land you own, the better your financial footing. Therefore, it's good to own residential and investment properties.

Two friends were driving home from fishing when one said to the other, "I forgot to buy my lottery ticket for tonight's drawing." He then asked his buddy to stop at the local convenience store so he could purchase what he hoped to be the winning ticket. "Why don't you save some time?" the friend asked. "As we pass the store, just throw your money out the window."

There's no need for us to try our luck at making money. Once we work for the money, we need to save and invest it and make our money work for us.

MANAGE YOUR MONEY: HOW TO KEEP IT

> If you want to build a tower, you first sit down and decide how much it will cost, to see if you have enough money to finish the job. If you don't, you might lay the foundation, but you would not be able to finish. Then all who would see it would make fun of you.
>
> —LUKE 14:28–29, NCV

Now that we understand money is a measure to honor God and a means to obtain a strong financial future, we must learn to manage it. This is where many fail. For some people, getting money is no problem, but keeping it is another matter.

Couples who come together in marriage without considering how their money will be managed are headed for trouble. A lady once asked me, "Should my husband and I split our finances fifty–fifty?" I responded by saying, "No."

I further explained the fifty-fifty rule expresses this: what's mine is mine, and what's yours is yours. There should be equality in the equity. The couple should see their finances as 100 percent theirs. There is no problem in having separate bank accounts, as long as there is a joint system to handle life's necessities. If you decide on having separate accounts, grant each other access. This extends trust to your spouse, as well as conveys you can be trusted.

In order to keep the money you make, utilize the *B*-word. *Budgeting* the bucks is the most effective way to keep what you earn and not waste it frivolously. To create a budget, start by knowing your debt-to-income ratio. I've heard it said, "If your *outflow* exceeds your *income*, your *upkeep* will become your *downfall*." A budget keeps us from spending more than we're bringing in.

It's imperative to know your *net income*. This is the income that actually comes into the house. Many marriages are suffering because one or both partners are trying to live off their gross income—above their means. These are people with good taste, but they don't taste good. In short, they spend money they don't have.

If your marriage is hemorrhaging financially, it's time to stop the bleeding. First, do your best to stop using credit cards for everything. These credit card lenders are hoping you'll fall victim to the world's system called compound interest. A good rule for using credit cards is this: if you can't repay the amount you used in thirty days, don't use it. Using cash for purchases allows you to spend moderately within your means.

I often hear people complain, "Life would be much easier if I received a raise." When given the chance, I advise these people to give themselves a raise. The way to give yourself a raise is by aggressively paying off debt. You can do this one or two ways: paying off the high-interest debt first (usually the preferred method) or paying off the amounts from least to greatest. Either way, the results are the same. The money that no longer goes to your lenders now goes into your pocket. Thus, you have just given yourself a financial raise.

Proper management of money allows us to accumulate wealth. This will give your family stability in these uncertain times. As you practice good management of money in good times you'll be better prepared in the hard times.

> The time eventually came when there was no food anywhere. The famine was very bad. Egypt and Canaan alike were devastated by the famine. Joseph collected all the money that was to be found in Egypt and Canaan to pay for the distribution of food. He banked the money in Pharaoh's palace. When the money from Egypt and Canaan had run out, the Egyptians came to Joseph. "Food! Give us food! Are you going to watch us die right in front of you? The money is all gone."
> —Genesis 47:13–15, The Message

Joseph was a man who knew how to manage money. Consequently, he was able to save nations from starvation and suffering. God used him to create a budget for Egypt that ultimately saved the lives of his loved ones.

Let's revisit the grasshopper and ant from our opening story. All summer the ant saved for the winter season as the grasshopper played the summer away.[2]

In the bitter cold the grasshopper declared, "I shall go share shelter and partake of the food belonging to the ant." Upon arriving at the ant's door the grasshopper requested lodging and a lunch.

The ant gave the grasshopper this stern reply: "All summer long I worked hard storing up food while you made fun of me. You invested nothing for the winter! Sorry grasshopper, but you must learn as you suffer." Then, the ant shut his door leaving the grasshopper out in the cold.

My friend, it is wise to consider tomorrow today. Have the right mind-set about your money by acknowledging it all belongs to God. Learn how to make your money grow so that it will eventually work for you. Finally, don't underestimate the importance of managing your money. It can make the difference between living your life in lack or abundance.

Remember, like the ant, if you pay now, you can play later. Make your money count.

THE LAUNDRY ROOM

A person might be an expert in any field of knowledge…
but without inner cleanliness his brain is a desert waste.
—SRI SATHYA SAI BABA[1]

Chapter Twelve

Come Clean

In 1895 America's major cities were steeped in muck and mire. New York alone had its streets barricaded with piles of animal and human waste. The situation in New York mirrored most of the country's condition.

Unsanitary disorder was the New York norm until city officials enlisted the aid of Col. George E. Waring. He was a Civil War veteran, legendary sewer engineer, and was dubbed the Apostle of Cleanliness. Waring was quickly assigned the head of New York's sanitation department.

With the monumental task of purifying the decomposing landscape, Waring recruited an army of two thousand sanitation workers in white uniforms. Many thought the task too difficult for Waring and his eco-warriors, while others claimed they were insane for even attempting the mop-up detail. Nevertheless, Waring was given the duty to disinfect the surrounding districts and that was exactly what he did.

His men cleaned four hundred and thirty-three miles of garbage from the streets. The city's rivers were recycled and sucked clean of most of its debris and grease. As a result of Waring's work, the city's death rate subsided, there was more usable water, and thousands of lives were saved.[2]

A really nice house comes equipped with a laundry room. Hardly anyone likes to air their dirty laundry, and there is no exception in marriage.

Fortunately, God has provided a method for couples to come clean without leaving their home. The method—the laundry room of our marriage—is called devotion. The old adage "The family that prays together stays together" holds a lot of truth. Even more, the couple that spends time in God's Word will become closer and invariably cleaner.

Daily devotion in God's Word allows us to have clean

heads to follow the Lord. It gives us clean hearts so we can trust the Lord. It gives us clean hands so that our work is acceptable unto the Lord. Cleanliness is next to godliness, and godliness keeps our marriages from becoming soiled and saturated in sin.

HAVING CLEAN HEADS

> Fix your thoughts on what is true and good and right. Think about things that are pure and lovely, and dwell on the fine, good things in others. Think about all you can praise God for and be glad about.
> —PHILIPPIANS 4:8, TLB

The thought of marriage paralyzes some people. I see it often. Couples come in my office for premarital counseling, and they stare at me like deer being hypnotized by headlights. Sure, they want marriage, but they are daunted by the many challenges matrimony presents.

These couples somehow expect me to give them all the answers to married life. They want to be given a road map to success that will allow them to scale prosperous peaks and avoid detrimental ditches.

For that reason, I tell them there is such a road map, a book that, if read, will disclose the mysteries of marriage. It reveals how to clear the dirt, clean the mind, and enables us to follow the Lord to green pastures. This book is the Bible, God's inspired Word for humanity.

When couples unite in holy matrimony they bring all their ideologies. Let's be honest and admit everything we learned is not correct. There are some habits that need halting, some attitudes that need adjusting, and some appetites that need to be abandoned.

This brings to mind a husband who enjoyed his wife's ham. After dinner he addressed his wife: "I love your ham, but tell me, why do you cut the ends off the meat?" The wife responded, "Well, my mother taught me how to prepare a ham, and she cut the ends off."

The following Thanksgiving holiday the entire family met for dinner at the wife's mother's house. True to form, the mother prepared a spectacular meal, which included her fabulous ham. After seeing the mother's ham, the husband noticed she cut the ends off her meat also. He enquired of his mother-in-law, "Why do you cut the ends off your ham?" She said, "Well, my mother taught me how to prepare a ham, and she always cut the ends off hers."

Now the husband was in total suspense, so he went to seek answers from the grandmother. "Grandma," he asked sheepishly, "why do you cut the ends off of your ham?" Grandma responded with a smile, "Honey, I have to cut the ends off my ham because my cooking pan is too short."

Sometimes we carry on traditions that needed to cease long ago. We could be cutting meat off our marriage because our minds need to be renewed. Only the Word of God can change our mind-set (Rom. 12:2). Couples must be cognizant to read God's Word together in order to grow as one. When a couple spends time in God's Word together it unifies their thought life and cleanses their mind.

> But I am afraid that your minds will be led away from your true and pure following of Christ just as Eve was tricked by the snake with his evil ways.
> —2 Corinthians 11:3 NCV

Having a clean mind allows us to follow God's Word. Someone wittingly gave the acronym for the Bible as "Basic instructions before leaving Earth." We must read the Word of God every day. The devil sets traps for us hoping we don't know God's Word. This is what happened to Adam and Eve.

The devil challenged Eve on the bases of God's Word. God said if they ate from the forbidden tree they would "*surely*" die (Gen. 2:16–17, emphasis added). When questioned by the devil, Eve replied that God said they shouldn't eat *or touch* the tree, "*lest*" they die (Gen. 3:2–3, emphasis added). Eve took away from God's Word because she did not say what God said—that they would surely die. She added to God's Word by saying, "He said don't touch the tree." God clearly didn't say that. Therefore, Eve changed God's Word. The results was the Fall and, with it, the filth. When we know God's Word, we are clean from the smut of the world and the dirt of the devil.

God's Word cleans a couple's thoughts, allowing them to think together, in one accord, and not become divided by the adversary. Not only do we need clean heads; we need clean hearts.

Having Clean Hearts

> So teach us to number our days, that we may apply our hearts unto wisdom.
>
> —Psalm 90:12

Over the years I have discovered many things, and one important fact is that God will never lead us where His grace cannot keep us. This is important when we're counting on God for a bright future. When we find ourselves lost it's not because God stops leading; it's because we stop following.

Having a clean heart allows us to trust the Lord completely. However, when our hearts are unclean we devise plans of our own. Authentic faith is not scheming; it's trusting God, no matter how the circumstance appears.

I'm sure you've heard people say, "Trust your heart; it won't lead you wrong." This is incorrect. The Bible says, "The heart is deceitful above all things, and desperately wicked: who can know it?" (Jer. 17:9). We must rely on God's Word to direct our path and pave His way.

The hardest judgment God can give us is our own way.

This is true because a man's ways seem right, but the end is death (Prov. 14:12).

God gave Israel their way when they protested for an earthly king and ended up with Saul, who was horrible (1 Sam. 8:6). God gave Israel their way when they cried for meat over His manna, and they had so much meat it was coming out of their noses (Num. 11:1–20). The best approach came from Jesus. Before surrendering His life on the cross, Jesus prayed to God the Father for a better way. However, He concluded His prayer by saying, "Thy will be done" (Matt. 26:42).

We must not allow our hearts to become polluted by not trusting the will of God. Couples who can no longer see eye to eye on issues and refuse to compromise with one another have allowed their hearts to become unclean. The Father's will is for couples to come together as one. His will is fulfilled as we read His Word.

God framed the world with His Word (Heb. 11:3). When darkness and the abyss encompassed the earth, He spoke His Word. His Word called light out of darkness (Gen. 1:2–3), life out of death (John 11:43–44), and can transform a marriage from filthy to fresh.

Our marriages thrive when we have faith in God. We maintain our faith through the devotion we place in reading His Word. Andrea and I share God's Word with each other as a source of encouragement. Everyone becomes weak at some point. However, in these times God's Word brings comfort. The suffix *fort* in *comfort* has Latin roots, namely *fortis*, meaning "strong."[3] God's Word gives us the strength we need to stay together and overcome any obstacles.

The Scriptures keep our hearts clean by ensuring we have faith in the Lord. Faith is integral in maintaining a pure heart. The Bible records God accepted Abel's offering, but He rejected Cain's (Gen. 4:4–5). Some have said Cain's offering was rejected because it was not sheep, like his brother Abel's, or because it was not given to God immediately. However,

Cain's offering was rejected because of his heart. Cain did not give to God in faith. In essence, Cain was not rejected because of his offering; his offering was rejected because of his heart. We know this because the Bible says, "By faith Abel offered unto God a more excellent sacrifice than Cain" (Heb. 11:4). Abel's offering was given in faith, and Cain's was not.

Beloved, get in God's Word with your spouse and offer your marriage to the Lord. Watch Him increase you in every way. The Bible provides a clear message that produces clean hearts, making it possible to follow the Father's will.

Consider the following poem by Perry Tanksley, which has been reproduced numerous times since 1984:

MARRIAGE TAKES THREE

I once thought marriage took
Just two to make a go
But now I am convinced
It takes the Lord also.
And not one marriage fails
Where Christ is asked to enter
As lovers come together
With Jesus at the center.
But marriage seldom thrives
And homes are incomplete
Till He is welcomed there
To help avoid defeat.
In homes where Christ is first
It's obvious to see
Those unions really work,
For marriage still takes three.[4]

HAVING CLEAN HANDS

> The righteous keep moving forward, and those with
> clean hands become stronger and stronger.
>
> —JOB 17:9, NLT

The greatest opportunity we have is to allow God to use us
to bless others. A greater privilege is when the Lord can use
you and your spouse together.

God's greatest gift to humanity is Jesus. The Father saw
the moral decadence of humanity and decided to send the
Son. To deliver His precious package God sought the assistance of Joseph and Mary. Through this couple He provided
the answer to humanity's problem.

This couple was not chosen on the basis of their perfection, because they were far from flawless. They were chosen
because their hands were clean. The Bible reveals May was a
virgin (Luke 1:27). This signified she was clean. Clean hands
are a prerequisite for handling God's business.

Neither Joseph nor Mary understood the whole plan of
God, but they learned to trust God through His Word. Mary
told the angel she would surrender according to God's Word
(Luke 1:38). Subsequently, she would deliver Jesus to the rest
of the world.

We must follow Mary's example to the fullest. God wants
to reveal Jesus through our marriage. In order for Him to do
this, He needs us to spend time in His Word. We are not able
to say, "Be it unto us according to God's Word," if we are not
aware of what His Word declares.

> Friendship with God is reserved for those who rever-
> ence him. With them alone he shares the secrets of his
> promises.
>
> —PSALM 25:14, TLB

Reading God's Word cleanses your hands; as a result, you become God's friend and, coincidently, friends with your spouse. It is important to have clean hands. Having clean hands means we are not into things that will bring shame to the name of the Lord. It also means our spouse can safely trust us.

When everyone else was busy performing wicked acts and having vile imaginations, God's wrath was kindled greatly. The entire Earth would have been annihilated if it had not been for one man—Noah. Genesis 6:9 tells us, "Noah walked with God." This indicates his hands were clean.

God looked from heaven and saw a world that was filled with dirt, stained by soot, and floundered in filth. He did what anyone does when they see dirt. He turned on the water. God then instructed Noah to build a boat for himself, his family, and some of God's creation.

The interesting thing is, Noah didn't build his boat for navigation; he built it to float. This indicated he would not try to direct his family's course but leave that option strictly to God. When our hands are clean our work is acceptable to God and our family's lives are the better for it.

Too often people take matters into their own hands. They call it getting their hands dirty. God doesn't want our hands dirty. He wants them clean. No matter the problems, we must place them in the hands of the Lord.

Sadly, I counsel too many couples that have their hands involved in matters that are not good. The Lord is the Good Shepherd (John 10:14), Great Shepherd (Heb. 13:20), and Chief Shepherd (1 Pet. 5:4), and He's looking to help His sheep. We are the sheep of His pasture, but we must be ever mindful not to act like pigs. There is a distinct difference between sheep and pigs. Sheep are not comfortable in dirt, but pigs enjoy filth.

When couples are not clean they can become accustomed

to a filthy lifestyle. At this point, they no longer enjoy their marriage. They merely endure it.

> Christ used the word to make the church clean by washing it with water.
> —EPHESIANS 5:26, NCV

Whenever there's a dirty issue in marriage, there's no need for panic. The laundry room is within reach. There we can remove any stain. We are made clean through the Word of God.

In 1895 Col. George Waring and his army of sanitation workers began the grueling task of cleaning up New York's filth. In his success he earned a reputation and established a recipe for our nation to follow.[5]

After Waring, many of America's cities integrated their waste efforts, and every large city in the nation eventually incorporated sewers. The fight against filth was taking a positive turn.

Our country is still in need of a good scrubbing. Our communities and families depend on good hygiene for survival. However, it all begins with my marriage and yours. So, for the sake of sanitation, don't just come together—come clean.

THE GARDEN

Never lose an opportunity of seeing anything beautiful,
for beauty is God's handwriting.
—Ralph Waldo Emerson

Chapter Thirteen

Smell the Roses

A man sat at a metro station in Washington DC and started to play the violin; it was a cold January morning. He played six Bach pieces for about 45 minutes. During that time, since it was rush hour, it was calculated that thousands of people went through the station, most of them on their way to work.

Three minutes went by and a middle aged man noticed there was a musician playing. He slowed his pace and stopped for a few seconds and then hurried up to meet his schedule. A minute later, the violinist received his first dollar tip: a woman threw the money in the till and without stopping continued to walk. A few minutes later, someone leaned against the wall to listen to him, but the man looked at his watch and started to walk again. Clearly he was late for work.

The one who paid the most attention was a three-year-old boy. His mother tagged him along, hurried but the kid stopped to look at the violinist. Finally the mother pushed hard and the child continued to walk turning his head all the time. This action was repeated by several other children. All the parents, without exception, forced them to move on.

In the forty-five minutes the musician played, only six people stopped and stayed for a while. About twenty gave him money but continued to walk their normal pace. He collected thirty-two dollars. When he finished playing and silence took over, no one noticed it. No one applauded, nor was there any recognition.

No one knew this but the violinist was Joshua Bell, one of the best musicians in the world. He played one of the most intricate pieces ever written with a violin worth 3.5 million dollars.

Two days before his playing in the subway, Joshua Bell

sold out at a theater in Boston and the seats averaged one hundred dollars.

Joshua Bell playing incognito in the metro station was organized by the *Washington Post* as part of a social experiment about perception, taste and priorities of people. Do we perceive beauty? Do we stop to appreciate it? Do we recognize the talent [and beauty] in an unexpected context?[1]

As we take care to cover the house of our marriage, there's one particular area that needs to be addressed, the garden. The garden is a place of beauty. However, the flowers in the garden must be cultivated in order for its loveliness to remain.

A house with a garden reveals something about the owners. It shows that they give attention to spectacles of beauty.

Like the garden, marriage is beautiful when the couple takes time to smell the roses. They must not take the garden of their marriage for granted. And they must realize it will not grow on its own but must be cultivated. The couple must be delicate, given to details, and devoted to each other.

WE MUST BE DELICATE

> He is able to deal gently with those who are ignorant and are going astray, since he himself is subject to weakness.
> —HEBREWS 5:2, NIV

In marriage, delicacy is mandatory. I'm not suggesting we tiptoe around our spouse and handle one another with kid gloves. I'm conveying we use gentleness.

Too often we modify what we say and our behavior around other people but lack consideration for our spouse. If our marriage is to reveal beauty, we must begin by being delicate with each other.

I love to see houses with gorgeous gardens, and when I do, I always say, "I'm going to grow my own garden." I enthusiastically buy the soil, plant food, and garden tools. I peruse the neighborhood greenhouses for the perfect flowers. I rush home and find the perfect spot to display beauty and perfection. Once the flowers are planted, I provide the suggested amount of water and hope the sun will do the rest.

At first, I sit and admire my flower garden, but soon, a myriad of duties demand my attention. I leave my garden with intentions to return. Some days later, I notice my flowers are fading more than flourishing.

Concerned, I return to the store to complain about receiving bad flowers only to discover the flowers were given a bad owner. The store clerk's instructions reveal a major part of my problem—*I am not delicate*. I'd rather feed my flowers a steady diet of Miracle Grow than take the time to help them grow.

There is no magical solution in marriage. No amount of marriage seminars, counseling sessions, or even books (like this one) can substitute for taking the time to appreciate your spouse.

True appreciation of our spouse equals delicacy in our marriage. I remember as a child, everyone's house had a china cabinet. This cabinet displayed the finest dinnerware for all to admire. Ironically, some people treat their possessions better than they treat their partner, which should never be the case. If we want our marriage to flourish, we must be careful to treat our spouse delicately. Never become so comfortable with your spouse that you take them for granted.

The rewards of delicacy cannot be overlooked. We find a biblical example through the story of Ahasuerus and Esther. Ahasuerus was the king of the greatest empire in the world of his day. His powerful empire expanded from India to Ethiopia (Esther 1:1). Esther was a humble Jewish girl whose beauty far excelled the other maidens in her region. Ahasuerus, smitten by Esther's beauty and spirit, chose her to be his queen.

As the story goes, Esther and her people were doomed

for total annihilation by the king's prime minister, an evil despot by the name of Haman. The king was totally unaware of the situation and the peril that his beloved queen faced. However, he was the only one with the authority to rescue the Jews.

Taking into consideration the dire situation, Esther sought an audience with the king and was granted her petition. She did not rush into the king's presence complaining about her critical condition. Instead, she invited both the king and evil Haman to a dinner. At the dinner she still reserved bringing up the horrific topic. Esther chose to wait until the following evening at a second dinner to present the bad news. Some may say she was using diplomacy, but not so; she was treating the situation delicately.

By waiting she allowed God to intervene providentially. The night after the first dinner, the king was unable to sleep. He called for the royal records to be read to him and discovered that Mordecai (Esther's cousin) had saved his life and received no reward for his deed. This set the stage for the events that would occur at the second dinner.

At dinner the following evening, the king was so delighted in Esther, he told her to make any request, and it would be granted. Esther was careful how she answered the king and requested that her life and the life of her people be spared. Befuddled, the king inquired as to what she meant. This was when she exposed Haman's evil plot to destroy the Jews. In the end, the king ordered Haman killed and issued a decree allowing the Jews to protect themselves from their enemies.

Being delicate means employing God's wisdom in your marriage. Wisdom is to know what to do, how to do it, and most importantly, when it should be done. Like Esther, we need to wait on God in certain situations involving our marriage. When we are delicate, God's hand is deliberate, and our marriage is not in danger of decay.

WE MUST BE GIVEN TO DETAILS

"What's the matter, Hannah?" Elkanah would exclaim.
"Why aren't you eating? Why make such a fuss over
having no children? Isn't having me better than having
ten sons?"
—1 SAMUEL 1:8, TLB

Many marriages suffer due to one or both partner's lack of
attention to details. By details I am referring to the role each
partner plays to hold the marriage together. Paying attention to details can be as simple as detecting your spouse's
emotional state. When marital partners refuse to regard one
another's feelings, the union will slowly erode.

When counseling couples, many wives report that their
husbands have lost interest in how they feel and what
they think. These wives maintain that their husbands
have become distant in their communication and in some
instances neglect communicating altogether.

A majority of husbands report that their wives have become
more concerned with the children's needs than with theirs.
They complain that their wife spends more time at work or
with household chores, leaving little energy for intimacy.

In these cases, both partners are yearning for connection and/or affection from the other. In short, the details are
being ignored.

One day a poor aged man died. He had not amassed a
great fortune, but he wanted to leave all his earthly goods to
his son, who he loved dearly. The son had little respect for his
father and even less for the possessions his dad bequeathed
to him. Therefore, he decided to hold a garage sale and give
everything away for next to nothing.

A couple seeking to furnish their new home discovered an
antiquated painting among the items being displayed. They
gave the son twenty dollars for the painting but later decided
to have it appraised. They were flabbergasted to discover

the painting was valued at just over one hundred thousand dollars.

The son had great wealth in his possession but didn't recognize the value and lost it. The couple acquired great wealth because they tended to details.

When we recognize the details that matter to our spouse, we become exposed to a wealth of love and companionship. The Bible says everything God made was good. He created you and your partner with the intricate details needed to enhance the beauty of your marriage.

Ma'am, right now you might see a frog, but look closer and discover he's a prince. Sir, you may think she's an ugly duckling, but check again and realize she's a swan. Amazingly, this person who you have trouble connecting with is the same person you married. In the beginning all you could see was potential. Could it be the only thing bad is your perception?

Mister, stop focusing on the fact that she gained weight and start realizing it's not always easy to lose pounds after childbearing. Look at the details of how she nurtures the children, cooks your meals, washes clothes, cleans the house, and still goes to work.

Ma'am, stop complaining he's not making enough money or he doesn't communicate on your level. Notice that he is there for the children, provides the money for household expenses, orders take-out when you're too tired to cook, and attends church with the family.

The aforementioned details are mere examples of things we can underappreciate and overlook. Every couple has their own unique situation; however, failing to pay attention to the details can produce damaging results.

Look for the details; it will make your spouse happy and your marriage healthy.

WE MUST BE DEVOTED

My beloved is mine and I am his.
—SONG OF SOLOMON 2:16, NIV

True devotion stems from a heart of love. While love is the heartbeat of marriage, devotion holds everything together. Devotion enables the garden of your marriage to experience tremendous growth.

No one is devoid of love; albeit, we don't always project our love in the right place. We're supposed to love people and use things. However, many use people and love things. Some even use people to get the things they love. To love things and not your spouse is planting your love and devotion in the wrong place.

Some are facing divorce because they are not devoted to their marriage. This was the problem with the very first couple. The devil approached Eve with the temptation of the forbidden tree. She looked at the tree and saw that it was "good for food," "pleasant to the eyes," and could make her wise (Gen. 3:6). Rather than focusing on her union with her husband Adam, she was fixated on the things she could possess. For many people, the problem is not with having things; they want things they don't have. God told Adam and Eve they could eat of every tree in the garden with the exception of one (Gen. 2:16–17). Who can refute an offer of "all but one"? I'll tell you who: those who say, "All or nothing!"

Adam and Eve's lack of devotion to God caused a decline in their devotion to each other. The result could have cost them their marriage. Many are desire-driven, not motivated by dedication. Rather than being devoted to things, our devotion should belong to God and our spouse.

In my hometown of Philadelphia, Pennsylvania, we have parking meters. These are city-wide devices used to collect money for parking a particular length of time. When the time allotted for parking has expired, more tokens must be inserted into the machine if the driver desires to keep that parking space. This analogy is relevant to our marriage. In order to keep our marriage cultivated, we must insert tokens of devotion. The little things we do make huge impacts.

Let us revisit our opening account of the "poet of the violin," Joshua Bell. Remember, he is one of the world's most celebrated violinists. He continues to enchant audiences with his breathtaking virtuosity, tone of sheer beauty, and charismatic stage presence. Wherever he goes he gives sell-out performances.

Yet, as he played brilliantly at a metro station in Washington, DC, people hardly noticed he was there. "Just another pan-handler," so they thought, thereby taking for granted the world-renowned virtuoso who graced them with his presence.

If we do not have a moment to stop and listen to one of the best musicians in the world playing the best music ever written, how many other things are we missing in the garden of our marriage?

The three most significant impacts to humanity's existence took place in gardens. First, the fall of humanity happened in the Garden of Eden (Gen. 2:8); second, Jesus surrendered to the will of God in the garden of Gethsemane (Matt. 26:36-39; John 18:1); and third, there will be a time of peace and restoration in the glorious garden city (Rev. 21–22).

Please, don't take the garden of your marriage for granted. When it comes to your spouse, be delicate, pay attention to the details, and give them your true devotion.

Your marriage is your garden, so take time to smell the roses.

> Awake, north wind, and come, south wind! Blow on
> my garden, that its fragrance may spread everywhere.

Let my beloved come into his garden and taste its choice fruits.

—Song of Solomon 4:16, NIV

THE GARAGE

Each life is made up of mistakes and learning, waiting
and growing, practicing patience and being persistent.
—BILLY GRAHAM

Chapter Fourteen

Park It

ROME BOASTS A remarkable tale of dominance and growth and is steeped in rich history. It took thousands of years, but Rome grew from a small Latin village to a vast dominate empire. It earned a reputation of excellence for its building structures and the construction of its roads.[1]

At the height of its glory, Rome exacted its might on the surrounding Mediterranean regions, forcing them to submit to the Roman way of life. Eventually, the rulers of the Roman Empire thought it wise to stretch their reach farther, and this decision ultimately brought about their demise.

Undoubtedly, Rome's strength came from her military. However, the Roman military was built to fight against other armies, not entire countries. Therefore, as the regiments were dispersed it became increasingly difficult to maintain communication and the supplying of resources.

Ultimately, ancient Rome was torn apart through crooked politics, greed, and internal struggle. Notwithstanding, Rome left an indelible mark on many civilizations that adopted many of the Roman practices as their way of life, our United States included.

With all its splendor and rich history, we can see why Rome wasn't built in a day. This is a token of wisdom usually issued to those who forget that anything worth having is worth the wait. It also serves as a good catalyst for this chapter. It took centuries and the amalgamation of cultures and countless resources to construct Rome, but above all it took patience.

In this chapter we will look at the garage of marriage. I'm using the garage as a place of pause. People utilize their garages in various ways. However, the purpose of the garage is to park your car. Now there's a concept many tend to lack in marriage: the ability to park and pause.

Many are attempting to maneuver their marriages to success and are frustrated because their best efforts are coming up short. To those people the Lord is saying, "Park it."

Stop attempting to make something happen in your marriage and know the Lord has your marriage in the making. Figuratively speaking, "park it" means we don't have to take control; we can trust and wait on the Lord. Right now you may feel the need to make a decision or like time is running out, but don't panic—park.

WAIT FOR THE WORD

> I look to you, heaven-dwelling God, look up to you for help. Like servants, alert to their master's commands, like a maiden attending her lady, We're watching and waiting, holding our breath, awaiting your word of mercy.
>
> —PSALM 123:1–2, THE MESSAGE

There is an insidious disease creeping into the marital union. This disease is divorce.

Couples are finding themselves facing divorce more than ever before. Is divorce the result of new problems and pressures that our forefathers never had to contend with? Of course not. The Bible clearly states there is nothing new under the sun (Eccles. 1:9). Divorce is not new, and the root of it is hardness of heart. Only God's Word can soften the heart and restore life to the marriage.

Without exception, all of the couples I have counseled considering divorce have admitted to not reading God's Word on their own to receive an answer for their plight. Sure, many of them attend church regularly, but they fail to seek God's mind concerning their marriage in their private devotion, if they have intimate devotion in His Word at all.

My desire is not to attack anyone, nor is it to convey reading the Word of God exempts any of us from life's pain, problems, and pressures. Remember, overall, God's Word is not a prevention; it's a protection. Everyone is exposed to the winds of adversity, but the Word of God provides the strength necessary to stand and not be swept away.

God fed the children of Israel food from heaven that He called manna. Along with the manna, the Lord gave Moses specific instructions on how and when His people were to eat. God commanded the people to eat the manna early in the morning and not to save any for the next day.

If the people did not get up early to receive the manna, it would evaporate. This was to ensure that the people would not be lazy but would rise early to receive from the Lord. If they attempted to save their meal for the next day it would decay. This forced the people to place their faith in God every day and receive Him as their daily bread.

Today God's manna is His Word. And just as it was then, it is for us now. We are to seek God's Word early and not settle for reading it a few times a week. We must read God's Word every day; He must be our daily bread. A day without God's Word is a day in decay.

> A merry heart doeth good like a medicine: but a broken spirit drieth the bones.
>
> —Proverbs 17:22

God's Word is like medicine. Reading the Word of God gives us joy, because in it are the answers to life's struggles. People who read the Bible daily confess to having an inner peace that those who fail to devote their time to the Scriptures don't.

When I counsel those with troubled marriages, I share the wisdom that comes from reading God's Word. Some have even said, "I wish my marriage could be like yours." To that I reply, "Every marriage is different, because we are all different. However, we can all experience God's love, peace, grace, etc."

I further expound on marital illnesses. The problem for many is they don't know they're sick. We all are sick! Some of us are sick *with* something, some are sick *of* something, and others have a case of both. We all are sick. However, there are those who choose to properly use the prescribed medication, while others don't.

God's Word is the medicine. So, before starting your day or dealing with your spouse, wait on the Word. You might be surprised. A Word a day keeps the divorce attorneys away.

WAIT FOR THE WILL

> Father, if thou be willing, remove this cup from me: nevertheless not my will, but thine, be done.
> —LUKE 22:42

The key to ultimate success in marriage, family, career, and life as a whole is being in the will of God. As I say this I realize many people see God's will as being abstract. If you are one of these people, understand the will of God is not some Da Vinci code we must crack in order to find fulfillment.

One afternoon a father told his son to turn the volume on the television down. In protest the boy complained he wanted the TV to remain loud. The father approached his son and gave this reprimand: "Son, if I'm happy, you've got a good chance of being happy." He further explained, "Your being upset changes nothing. However, if I get upset I can change your whole environment."

It's the same way with God. If we get upset, our situation may not change. Nevertheless, if our attitude gets the Lord upset there can be radical repercussions. Make no mistake; it behooves us to please God.

The desire to please the Lord places us on the path of discovering His will for our lives. Apart from His will we are left on our own, groping around through life in the dark. Those who refuse to wait on the will of God do so without knowing God has their best interest at heart.

> Beloved, I wish above all things that thou mayest prosper and be in health, even as thy soul prospereth.
> —3 JOHN 1:2

Marriages are faltering and failing at a record pace. People are swapping spouses like cars, trading in families like coupons, and turning from their domestic obligations. The reason usually given for the moral flop is a spouse's dissatisfaction. The reality usually never considered is God's dissatisfaction. The question for the child of God should not be, "Am I pleased?" It needs to be, "Is God pleased?"

When God is pleased, His will is done, and our lives are the better for it. Do you want God's best for your marriage and your life? If so, the only way to receive it is by surrendering. Like Jesus, we must trust God's will over our own (Luke 22:42). This means we must yield our goals and aspirations to His trust and care.

When the world had plummeted into chaos, God instructed Noah to build an ark. Where is your world and marriage right now? If they're moving in a downward spiral you may think of bailing, but in times like these God thinks of building.

Just as the Lord instructed Noah in graphic detail to build his boat, He instructs us how to build our marriages. Two things are of particular interest concerning Noah's boat.

First, the ark only had one window on it. The window was not on the rear of the boat so Noah could see where he'd been. It was not on the front of the vessel so he could view where he was headed. It was not even on the side of the ship, where Noah could appreciate his present affair. Interestingly, the window was placed at the craft's crest (Gen. 6:16).

God told Noah to install a sun-roof. This way Noah would not focus on the conditions; he would focus on his God. Does the house of your marriage come equipped with a *Son*-roof? When things are not going the way you would like them, do you focus on the problem, or do you look up and consider your God?

The second peculiarity about Noah's ark was that it had no steering mechanism. This indicated that Noah would not rely on his own navigational prowess. He would look to God and lean strictly on the Lord's protection and direction.

When the forecast predicts a marriage monsoon, we must learn to surrender to God's will, trusting that He has our best interest at heart. When dark skies reside over your house, resist the temptation to relocate. Don't panic. Pause, be still, and know even though the clouds are dark, the sun is still shining, and God's Son will shine and show Himself.

My friend, the safest place for Noah was not the ark. It was God's will. In God's will we find rest from every storm. God said, "Enter into my rest" (Heb. 4:9–11, author's paraphrase). Whether it was Noah entering the boat or us entering our marriage, there's safety and security in God's rest. Now, we must learn to wait, because in our waiting, we win.

Remember, the will of God never leads us where the grace of God cannot keep us. Once you come to discover God's will for your marriage, it's imperative you do it God's way.

WAIT FOR THE WAY

> He made known his ways unto Moses, his acts unto the children of Israel.
>
> —PSALM 103:7

It would be great to have the Lord renew your marriage. Even better, you can learn how to renew your marriage yourself. Many people pray and ask God to act on their behalf.

However, God is looking for us to learn His ways so we can avoid marital meltdowns and elude negative nuptials.

God made known His acts unto the children of Israel, but His ways unto Moses. Why only His acts to the children of Israel? Maybe because all their lives they were referred to as children. Moses was mature, so he was privy to God's ways. Do you want to see God act, or are you interested in knowing His ways?

I recall spilling a cherry fruit drink on my wife's light-colored Berber carpet. I thought she would erupt and rake me over the coals. She erupted, but with elation. Turns out, my spill gave her opportunity to spend. Andrea desired wood floors, and she saw my clumsiness as a calling. My downfall became her upgrade.

Luckily, I caught a break. A friend of mine installs floors as a craft. He told me if I paid for the materials he would go beyond installing the floors; he would teach me how to place the floors in myself. First I was reluctant, but he ensured me that he would guide me every step of the way.

Sure enough, in a matter of a few days I had completed the job. Saving a few hundred dollars was great, but learning the ways to lay my floors was far better. There is an old adage that goes, "Give a man a fish, and you'll feed him for a day; teach him to fish, and you'll feed him for a lifetime."

While installing the flooring, my friend was patient with me. I asked hundreds of questions, and he answered them all. I made even more mistakes, and he came behind me and made the corrections. Through it all he continued to remind me, "You're learning. Keep going. Eventually you'll get the hang of it." And I did.

The entire process was exciting and frightening. At times I thought of the money and hours spent, and above all, I didn't want to disappoint Andrea, who could hardly wait to try out her new floors.

Now, looking back, I can say the greatest thing I gained

from this experience was the ability to wait. There were times when I felt I could speed up the process, but I had to learn patience and allow my friend's expertise to govern the task.

A good virtue to have in any marriage is patience. Patience reveals an inward ability to park. The Bible teaches us there is a season and time for everything (Eccles. 3:1). We just need to wait on the Lord.

> But they that wait upon the LORD shall renew their strength; they shall mount up with wings as eagles; they shall run, and not be weary; and they shall walk, and not faint.
>
> —ISAIAH 40:31

When we wait on the Lord He will reveal His way. His way far exceeds our own. The Bible declares there is a way that seems right to us, but the end is death (Prov. 14:12; 16:25). In fact, one of the harshest judgments God can give us is our own way.

Israel complained about wanting a mortal king instead of the Lord God Almighty (1 Sam. 8:6–7). The result was they received crazy King Saul. There was also a time when Israel griped about God's manna because they wanted meat. God gave them flesh until it was coming out their nostrils (Num. 11:18–20). Who can forget how Jonah went his own way, and it almost cost him his life (Jon. 1). In short, going our own way is detrimental.

God's way is not always easier, but make no mistake—it's better. We must learn to trust that He knows and wants what's best for us.

> I say this because I know what I am planning for you," says the LORD. "I have good plans for you, not plans to hurt you. I will give you hope and a good future.
>
> —JEREMIAH 29:11, NCV

The saying "Rome wasn't built in a day" is certainly an understatement. Today it is an international political and cultural center, a major global city, and is regarded as one of the most beautiful cities of the ancient world.

Something so breathtaking couldn't be constructed in a day or even a lifetime. The joy is in witnessing the miniscule transformed into the magnificent, the subpar into the sublime.

The next time things aren't going right in your marriage, wait for God's word, surrender to the Lord's will, and seek His way.

Rome wasn't built in a day, and neither will your marriage be completely built in a day. However, don't panic. Park with the knowledge you will reap a good harvest if you don't quit.

Epilogue

No Place Like Home

"THERE'S NO PLACE like home." You're probably familiar with that phrase. It was made popular by the 1939 classic *The Wizard of Oz*. For most of us the movie conjures up fond memories of a scarecrow who wanted a brain, a tin man who wanted a heart, and a lion who wanted courage. But for the main character, Dorothy, all she wanted was to go home.

You see, Dorothy woke up as she did every other morning and went about her day, but by day's end an unexpected storm struck her house. Its adverse winds carried her and her dog, Toto, far away from home. She awoke to find herself in a strange land among strange people.

Following the yellow brick road on her way to Oz, Dorothy encountered myriad tests and trials—from flying monkeys to wicked witches—but she would not be detoured. Neither did the hard times diminish her aspiration for home. Instead of depreciating, her home appreciated in value with each passing day, up to the day she tapped her heels three times and, with all the wishing she could muster, said with bated breath, "There's no place like home." She awoke in the safety of its dwelling.

A couple had been married for twenty-three years. One day the husband told his wife he was moving out, that he didn't want to be married anymore and he needed some space. Several weeks later she was served with a petition for divorce. Devastated, she felt like the winds of a tornado had flung her into her own personal Oz. Like a thunderclap in a storm, the words of the petition rumbled loudly through her mind, but instead of allowing the petition to speak, she cried out to the Lord. She laid that petition on the floor before the Lord, prostrated herself, and began to decree

2 Kings 19, treating that petition as Hezekiah did the words of Sennacherib.

Day after day the wife walked into her home after work, longing for what used to be. Her husband was on the other side of the world longing for the same thing, because there's no place like home. They both experienced feelings of being displaced, because although they had a physical roof over their head, they were exiled from their marital home.

After the divorce the husband, realizing he was living in a state of quasi-homelessness, began to yearn for his wife. Willing to do whatever it took to get her back, he started calling his ex-wife, and his visits home became more and more frequent. Whenever they were together there was the feeling of belonging, of safety, and security within the walls they had built together.

Do I really need to finish the story? You know what happened, don't you? The ex-husband began to date his ex-wife again, and things picked up where they left off. The architectural detail of their home remained intact, but they added new love features that certainly appreciated its value. What seemed to be a condemned structure, in reality, had solid bones. Hence, their beautiful, old home just needed a little maintenance; it just needed to be repaired.

Throughout this book marriage is typed as a house where husbands and wives dwell intimately and securely within its walls. But what happens when violent storms assail and leave it pillaged and plundered, followed by the enemy pilfering what remains? In such a state of disrepair many couples think all hope is lost and so abandon the remnants to the elements. But don't be so quick to hang out that Condemned sign. I submit to you that your house can indeed be restored to its former glory! In fact, the Lord promises in Joel 2:25, "And I will restore to you the years that the locust hath eaten, the cankerworm, and the caterpillar, and the palmerworm."

Did you notice the term *years*? That means no matter how

long the house has been sitting in disrepair, the Lord will restore! The locust, cankerworm, caterpillar, and palmerworm show a progression of devastation, of nibbling away until everything is completely devoured. But the Lord *still* says, "I will restore."

John Gill's Exposition of the Bible interprets the Hebrew words translated "I will restore" (*shalam*) as follows:

> I will recompense to you the years; give you fruitful ones, as a full compensation for those in which the locust ate up the fruits of the earth for some years running.[1]

It reminds me of an old Victorian house, decrepit and abandoned. Restoring such a house not only refurbishes its beauty but also increases its value and standing in the neighborhood, with its history intact. To restore a marriage, God restores both husband and wife to their proper standing. He restores the beauty of their history—the good, the bad, and the ugly; the flying monkeys; and wicked witches—all working synergistically with the present to bring about a greater appreciation for what they built together.

That sort of appreciation is sorely lacking in today's society. We live in an era of technological advances. We are so into upgrades and caught up on the latest gadgets because we think the latest is the greatest. We want the latest iPhone, Android, Mac, and PC. We throw away things simply because they're old or outdated. This attitude is even creeping into our marriages. In our quest to pursue that which is newer, younger, we begin to look at our spouse as if a wrinkle implies a loss of value.

Well, newer is not always better. It is sometimes just cheaper. The late Ed Cole astutely called it "high gloss; cheap material." To have a home of true value there must be an assertive effort to keep it up. Home is where the heart is, but where is your state of mind? If home is where the heart is, it follows that no matter where you are—whether a tiny condo or a two-hundred-fifty-year-old colonial—if your heart is right, your home is indissoluble. It's flood-proof, stormproof, enemy-proof. That is why we must assume the posture of one prepared to stay for the long haul—'til death do us part. We've got to dig in until the storm passes and the reparation is complete.

Did I finish the story about that couple? Not only are they happily *remarried*, but their sons went on to successful lives. One is married with children and coaching at a school. The other went on to the NFL. God indeed restored their years, just as He promised, and the glory of their latter house is greater than their former house.

Perhaps you have some Sennacheribs prophesying destruction to your marriage. Or maybe there are some wicked witches and flying monkeys opposing your journey homeward. Don't abandon your dwelling place. Don't give up hope. Instead, tap your heels together three times for the Trinity and declare the Word of the Lord in Joel 2:25: "And I will restore to you the years that the locust hath eaten." Set your heart to go the distance. Don't *replace*; *repair*, knowing the Lord will give you full compensation for the years the locusts devoured because *there's no place like home.*

Notes

CHAPTER TWO:
THE FURNACE OF AFFLICTION

1. "Biography," *NelsonMandela.org*, Nelson Mandela Foundation, accessed August 20, 2014, at http://www.nelson mandela.org/content/page/biography.
2. "National Marriage and Divorce Rate Trends," *Centers for Disease Control and Prevention*, accessed July 20, 2014, at http://www.cdc.gov/nchs/nvss/marriage_divorce_tables.htm.
3. "Biography," *NelsonMandela.org*.

CHAPTER FOUR:
A MESSAGE IN THE MESS

1. Noah Webster, Ed., *American Dictionary of the English Language*, 1828 Facsimile First Edition (Chesapeake, VA: Foundation for American Christian Education, 1967, 1995), s.v. "baggage."

CHAPTER FIVE:
twONE

1. "Jan. 5, 1933: Construction Begins on Golden Gate Bridge," *The History Channel*, accessed July 20, 2014, at http://www .history.com/this-day-in-history/construction-begins-on -golden-gate-bridge.
2. Matrix inspired by Robert J. Morgan, "Communication in Marriage," *Nelson's Complete Book of Stories, Illustrations, and Quotes* (Nashville, TN: Thomas Nelson, 2000), 135.
3. "Jan. 5, 1933: Construction Begins on Golden Gate Bridge," *The History Channel*.

CHAPTER SIX:
THE REST OF THE STORY

1. "October 30, 1974: Muhammad Ali wins the Rumble in the Jungle," *History.com*, accessed October 21, 2014, at http:// www.history.com/this-day-in-history/muhammad-ali-wins -the-rumble-in-the-jungle.

2. Dennis Thompson Jr., "Health Risks of Long-Term Sleep Deprivation," *Everyday Health*, accessed October 21, 2014, at http://www.everydayhealth.com/sleep/health-risks-of -long-term-sleep-deprivation.aspx.
3. William Holmes McGuffey, "Lesson XLVI," *McGuffey's Eclectic Primer, Revised Edition*, Ed. Don Kostuch, *Project Gutenberg*, accessed August 20, 2014, at http://www.guten berg.org/files/14642/14642-pdf.pdf.
4. "October 30, 1974: Muhammad Ali wins the Rumble in the Jungle," *History.com*.

Chapter Seven:
Check Yourself

1. "William Henry Harrison," *History.com*, accessed October 21, 2014, at http://www.history.com/topics/us-presidents/ william-henry-harrison.
2. "45 Best Health Tips Ever," *Health24*, accessed July 21, 2014, at http://www.health24.com/Medical/Flu/Health-tips/45- best-health-tips-ever-20120721.
3. Ibid.
4. Ibid.
5. Edward K. Rowell and Bonne L. Steffen, Eds., *Humors for Preaching and Teaching from Leadership Journal and Christian Reader* (Ada, MI: Baker Publishing Group, 1996).
6. "William Henry Harrison," *History.com*.

Chapter Eight:
At Your Service

1. "Biography Mother Teresa," *Biography Online*, accessed August 21, 2014, at http://www.biographyonline.net/nobel- prize/mother_teresa.html.
2. "Eugene Allen," *Biography*, A&E Television Networks, accessed August 21, 2014, at http://www.biography.com/ people/eugene-allen-21095473#synopsis.
3. William Holmes McGuffey, "Lesson VI," *McGuffey's Second Eclectic Reader*, Ed. Don Kostuch, *Project Gutenberg*, accessed August 20, 2014, at http://www.gutenberg.org/ cache/epub/14668/pg14668.html.
4. "Eugene Allen," *Biography*.

CHAPTER NINE:
BIRDS OF A FEATHER

1. Melissa Mayntz, "Why Birds Flock," *About.com*, accessed August 24, 2014, at http://birding.about.com/od/birdbehavior/a/Why-Birds-Flock.htm.
2. Victor Hugo quote referenced in Elaine Sommers Rich, *Breaking Bread Together* (Eugene, OR: Wipf & Stock Pub, 2007), 71.

CHAPTER TEN:
FOCUS, PLEASE!

1. Jennifer Rosenberg, "Alexander Fleming Discovers Penicillin," *About.com*, accessed August 20, 2014, at http://history1900s.about.com/od/medicaladvancesissues/a/penicillin.htm.
2. Dr. Howard Markel, "The Real Story Behind Penicillin," *PBS Newshour*, accessed August 24, 2014, at http://www.pbs.org/newshour/rundown/the-real-story-behind-the-worlds-first-antibiotic/.
3. Leslie B. Flynn, quoted at "Bible, Inerrancy of," *Sermon Illustrations*, accessed August 24, 2014, at http://www.sermonillustrations.com/a-z/b/bible_inerrancy_of.htm.
4. Dr. Howard Markel, "The Real Story Behind Penicillin," *PBS Newshour*.

CHAPTER ELEVEN:
MAKING MONEY COUNT

1. Adapted from "The Ant and the Grasshopper," *Aesop's Fables*. Retelling available at http://www.civprod.com/storylady/stories/AesopFables.htm.
2. Ibid.

CHAPTER TWELVE:
COME CLEAN

1. Sri Sathya Sai Baba quote found at *Think Exist*, accessed August 24, 2014, at http://thinkexist.com/quotation/a-person-might-be-an-expert-in-any-field-of/351052.html.
2. *America: The Story of Us*, Disc 2, A&E Television Networks, 2010.

3. *Dictionary.com*, s.v., "comfort," accessed October 21, 2014, at http://dictionary.reference.com/browse/comfort.
4. Perry Tanksley, "Marriage Takes Three," Publisher unknown.
5. *America: The Story of Us,* Disc 2.

CHAPTER THIRTEEN:
SMELL THE ROSES

1. This article is from an often-distributed paraphrase of Gene Weingarten's *Washington Post* article "Pearls Before Breakfast" from April 8, 2007, which chronicles the Post's experiment on the willingness of commuters to stop and appreciate beauty. Weingarten's original article may be found at http://www.washingtonpost.com/wp-dyn/content/article/2007/04/04/AR2007040401721.html.

CHAPTER FOURTEEN:
PARK IT

1. "Ancient Rome," *History.com*, accessed October 21, 2014, at http://www.history.com/topics/ancient-history/ancient-rome.

EPILOGUE:
NO PLACE LIKE HOME

1. "Introduction to Chapter in Joel," *John Gill's Exposition of the Bible*, accessed October 21, 2014, at *GodRules.net,* http://www.godrules.net/library/gill/28gilljoe2.htm, s.v. "verse 25."

About the Author

TYRONE AND HIS wife, Andrea, have worked in full-time ministry for almost two decades. They serve under the tutelage of Bishop Nate Holcomb, the pastor and founder of Christian House of Prayer Ministries, Inc.

With a heart of compassion and a desire to impart learning, Tyrone Holcomb lays out the counsel of God with simplistic ease. He masterfully weaves biblical principles with humorous stories and witty phraseology that inspires laughter, while enabling the listener to grasp and apply the truths of God's Word. Personal experience has taught him, "What life does to you depends on what life finds in you." Hence, his endeavor is to ensure always that Christ is found in all that he does.

Tyrone and Andrea's firm conviction is that God is straight, God is strong, and God won't leave you stranded. Therefore, they confidently conclude: God's greatest ability is His dependability.

This anointed couple senses the call of God to strengthen and solidify today's marriages. With the understanding that marriage is a picture of Christ and His church, Tyrone Holcomb has authored three pragmatic books: *Marriage Matters: For Better or for Worse, Marriage Matters Vol. II: Learning to Love Like God*, and *Marriage Medicine: Character Is the Cure*.

He and Andrea use these resources to conduct marriage seminars and marital counseling. Moreover, their ministry extends beyond the subject of marriage, as they travel the country teaching and preaching the whole counsel of God.

Contact the Author

Tyrone Holcomb
P.O. Box 2542
Harker Heights, TX 76548

THOLCOMB@CHOP.ORG

(254) 547–1413

Like us on Facebook:
Tyrone Holcomb

Follow us on Twitter

@HolcombTyrone

IS YOUR MARRIAGE HEALTHY?

Make Your Marriage Matters

More Than Ever Before.

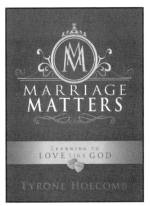

Tap into the good life God has provided for marriages. In *Marriage Matters* author and minister Tyrone Holcomb shows readers how to apply God's Word to learn to love their spouse in a whole new way, thereby weathering the storms that will inevitably challenge anyone's marriage. Readers will be able to rekindle their love for their spouse through kindness, overcome struggles through patience, develop a "community of unity," and most importantly, strengthen the pillar of trust. By taking the love that God has freely given to believers and administering that same love to their spouses, readers can recapture the mandate for every believer—to love unconditionally. The result will be an unbreakable bond and a marriage steeped in the good life of God.

Order Your Copy Today!